GREAT DISHES
for
CHILDREN

Quick, affordable
and lots of new ideas

ABBREVIATIONS

P	=	protein
tbsp	=	tablespoon(s)
F	=	fat
g	=	gram(s)
CH	=	carbohydrate
kcal	=	kilocalories
kg	=	kilogramme(s)
kJ	=	kilojoules
ml	=	millilitre(s)
tsp	=	teaspoon(s)

COMMON MEASURES

1 teaspoon (tsp)	=	5 ml
1 tablespoon (tbsp)	=	15 ml

Picture credits:
P. 4 bottom left, 17, 20, 25, 32, 35, 37, 40, 42–45, 52,
55, 57–60, 75 and 79: Fotostudio Klaus Arras
P. 5 top right, 98, 100, 104–106, 108, 109, 111–113,
115, 116, 119, 120 and 122: Klaus Klaussen
All other photos: TLC Fotostudio

Illustration credits:
All illustrations © LenLis – Fotolia.com

Contents

Introduction

Food for children must meet a number of requirements from the start: it should be tasty, look appetising and be easy to prepare so it can be on the table quickly when they are peckish or ravenous. However, it should also be healthy and provide children with the necessary minerals, vitamins, roughage, protein and trace elements. Does that sound like a lot? It certainly does, but it is also really easy. In this book you will find a large number of recipes that meet these requirements. At the same time, when selecting them we thought it was important to introduce you to new recipes and go beyond the same old "recipes for children" like spaghetti Bolognese and apple pancakes. The choice of recipes was guided by the idea of a healthy mixed diet.

Healthy mixed diet

A healthy diet is the best way of ensuring your children will be healthy and not suffer from obesity, tooth decay or deficiency symptoms. The prerequisite for this is a balanced, mixed diet containing all the important nutrients – proteins, minerals, vitamins, carbohydrates. With our delicious, varied meals spread throughout the day you will meet your child's nutritional needs and bring variety to the family table.

Children develop their own tastes very early on but parents have every opportunity to guide their preferences for particular foods and also their eating habits. If adults and elder brothers and sisters set a good example with regard to nutrition, a child will very soon come to think of healthy eating as the norm.

The value of everyday meals is already decided by the choice of the most basic foods. Wholemeal bread, crispbread and rolls should have priority on the table, rather than white bread and rolls made from pale wheat flour. We have avoided so-called "empty calories" as provided by sugar and superfine flour, and natural rice and wholewheat noodles are real alternatives along with rice and pasta. One little tip: include your child as far as possible in the preparation of the food. Even cooked food is much more likely to be tried if it contains ingredients or combinations that are unfamiliar to the child.

Mealtimes

Eating habits vary from family to family, so we have not subdivided meals into lunch and evening meals but instead we have only made a distinction between light dishes and main dishes. The time at which the main meal is eaten is basically of secondary importance. Nevertheless, you should take care not to eat too late. The evening meal should be eaten at least two hours before bedtime so that it does not hinder refreshing sleep. Because children cannot store large amounts of energy, in addition to breakfast, lunch and an evening meal, they should also have a sandwich or two at break time in the morning and an afternoon snack. Nevertheless, this can differ widely and will depend on how much children eat at the three main mealtimes and how active they are.

That extra-special something

To ensure plenty of fun, in our third chapter we have assembled some very special recipes for you that will make your next children's party unforgettable. Cucumber crocodiles, sausage caterpillars and monster muffins – not only the children will be wide-eyed. Prepare to be surprised by all our great ideas.

Enjoy browsing through the book and cooking and eating together.

Snacks and small dishes

Small dishes are ideal, when an apple or vegetable sticks to nibble between meals are not enough – or if children are not very hungry at lunchtime or in the evening. Soups, muffins, quiches and many more mean that there is always something to suit every taste. We have even included a few sweet dishes.

Cheese soup

zuppa di fontina

Serves 4

100 g wafer-thin slices of bread,
400 g fontina cheese, 1 ¹/₄ litres meat stock

Quick

1 Toast the slices of bread in a dry pan and place one in each of 4 soup bowls – if possible with lids. Slice the cheese very thinly and lay it on the bread.

2 Add alternate layers of bread and cheese slices until all have been used up.

3 Bring the meat stock to the boil and pour over the bread and cheese mixture. Cover the soup bowls, stand them in a hot oven to draw for approx. 5 minutes and serve immediately.

Preparation time: approx. 20 minutes (plus approx. 5 minutes to draw)
Per portion approx. 446 kcal/1868 kJ; 29 g P, 29 g F, 15 g CH

Semolina dumpling soup

Serves 4

60 g butter, 2 eggs, 125 g Durum wheat semolina, salt, 1 pinch ground nutmeg,
1 tbsp oil, 1 litre vegetable stock, 3 tbsp freshly chopped chives

1 Heat the butter in a pan and stir until foamy. Add the eggs, then gradually add the semolina and mix well. Season the mixture with salt and nutmeg and leave to swell for about 1 hour.

2 Brush a plate with oil. Then scoop out small balls of dumpling mixture with a teaspoon and put them on the plate. Leave to rest for about 15 minutes.

3 Simmer the dumplings in plenty of boiling salted water over low heat for about 10 minutes, until they have doubled in size. Then scoop out with a slotted spoon and leave to drain.

4 Heat the vegetable stock in a second pan and add the dumplings. Sprinkle with chives and serve.

Preparation time: approx. 20 minutes (plus approx. 1 hour to swell, approx. 15 minutes to rest and approx. 10 minutes to draw)
Per portion approx. 265 kcal/1113 kJ; 5 g P, 17 g F, 22 g CH

Pancake soup

Serves 4

1 onion, 1 leek, 2 carrots, $1/4$ celeriac, 400 g stewing steak, 1 tbsp sunflower oil, $1 1/2$ litres vegetable stock, salt, pepper, 1 bay leaf, 2 eggs, 150 g flour, 175 ml milk, 2 tbsp butter, 1 bunch chives

1 Peel the onion and chop finely. Trim, wash and dry the leek and chop roughly. Wash, peel, trim and slice the carrots. Wash, trim and dice the celeriac. Rinse the meat, pat dry and cut in rough pieces.

2 Heat the sunflower oil in a large pan, lightly brown the onion and vegetables. Add the meat and then immediately add the cold vegetable stock. Add a teaspoon of salt, pepper and the bay leaf. Cover and simmer for $1 1/2$ hours.

3 For the pancakes, beat the eggs, flour and milk together with a pinch of salt until smooth. If the batter is too runny, beat in more flour. Melt a little butter in a pan and add a small ladleful of batter. Fry the pancakes on both sides until golden yellow and roll up and cut in slices while still hot. Continue until all the batter has been used.

4 Wash the chives, pat dry and cut in rings. Sieve the soup and season the bouillon to taste with salt and pepper. Arrange the pancakes in soup plates and pour over the bouillon. Sprinkle with chives and serve.

Preparation time: approx. 35 minutes (plus approx. 1 hour 30 minutes cooking time)
Per portion approx. 280 kcal/1170 kJ; 29 g P, 12 g F, 14 g CH

Fried mozzarella sandwiches

Serves 4

200 g mozzarella, 8 pieces white bread (about the same size as the mozzarella), 2 eggs, 1 tbsp milk, salt, pepper, a little flour for tossing, 5 tbsp olive oil

Crispy

1 Cut the mozzarella into 4 slices and place each on a slice of white bread of about the same size. Top each with a second slice of bread, making sure the mozzarella does not hang over the edges of the bread. Briefly dip the edges of the bread in cold water then press them together.

2 Beat the eggs and milk in a shallow bowl and season with salt and pepper. Tip the flour onto a plate. Toss the sandwiches first in flour, then in the egg mixture. Heat the oil in a pan and fry the mozzarella sandwiches on both sides until crisp. Serve hot.

Preparation time: approx. 10 minutes (plus approx. 10 minutes frying time)
Per portion approx. 249 kcal/1045 kJ; 14 g P, 20 g F, 4 g CH

Tuna and courgette muffins

Makes 12

185 g tuna in oil (tinned), 400 g courgettes, $^1/_2$ yellow pepper, 150 g mozzarella, 250 g flour, 2 $^1/_2$ tsp baking powder, $^1/_2$ tsp bicarbonate of soda, 1 egg, 60 ml olive oil, 200 g natural yoghurt, salt, pepper, $^1/_2$ tsp dried rosemary, fat for greasing

1 Drain the tuna and divide into pieces. Wash, trim, dry and grate the courgettes. Trim, wash, dry and dice the pepper. Dice the mozzarella. Pre-heat the oven to 180 °C (Gas Mark 4). Grease a muffin tin.

2 Mix the flour with the baking powder and bicarbonate of soda. Mix the egg with the olive oil and natural yoghurt. Fold in the tuna, courgettes and mozzarella. Season with salt and pepper and mix in the rosemary. Mix together with the flour to give a smooth dough.

3 Spoon the dough into the muffin tins and bake on the middle shelf of the oven for approx. 25 minutes. Leave to rest in the oven for 5 minutes, then remove the muffins from the tins and leave to cool completely on a wire rack.

Preparation time: approx. 20 minutes
(plus approx. 25 minutes baking time)
Per muffin approx. 201 kcal/844 kJ; 9 g P, 10 g F, 16 g CH

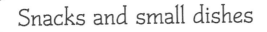
Club sandwich
with turkey

Serves 4

4 rashers bacon, 4 tbsp mayonnaise, 2 tsp lemon juice, 1 tsp mustard, salt, pepper, 8 slices white bread, 8 leaves iceberg lettuce, 8 slices roast turkey breast, 4 slices Cheshire cheese, 4 cherry tomatoes

1 Fry the bacon in a dry, nonstick pan until crisp and leave to cool on kitchen roll. Mix together the mayonnaise, lemon juice, mustard, salt and pepper.

2 Toast the bread golden brown. Spread two-thirds of the mayonnaise on one side each of 4 slices of toast. Cut the iceberg lettuce in strips and arrange half of them on the toast. Place 2 slices of turkey breast and 1 slice of cheese on each. Top with the remaining slices of toast.

3 Spread with the remaining mayonnaise, top with strips of lettuce and bacon and cut the sandwiches in half diagonally. Pin each sandwich together with a toothpick and half a tomato.

Preparation time: approx. 20 minutes
Per portion approx. 313 kcal/1315 kJ; 17 g P, 16 g F, 26 g CH

Tuna toast

Serves 4

4 slices white bread, 4 tsp butter, 1 tin tuna in oil (185 g), 2 tomatoes, salt, pepper, 4 slices Gouda, 4 cherry tomatoes, 1 tbsp freshly chopped parsley

1 Pre-heat the oven to 225 °C (Gas Mark 7). Toast the bread until golden brown. Spread the toast with butter and place on a baking sheet lined with baking paper.

2 Drain the tuna thoroughly and pull apart. Wash, dry and trim the tomatoes and cut in slices. Arrange the tomato slices on the toast and season with salt and pepper. Spoon the tuna over the tomatoes and top with slices of cheese.

3 Bake in the oven until the cheese has melted. Cut the toast in half diagonally. Wash and dry the cherry tomatoes and cut in half. Top each triangle with half a cherry tomato. Sprinkle with parsley and serve.

Preparation time: approx. 10 minutes (plus approx. 5 minutes to gratinate)
Per portion approx. 353 kcal/1412 kJ; 14 g P, 27 g F, 12 g CH

Porcini mushroom and potato cake

Serves 12

125 g low-fat quark, 3 tbsp milk, 4 tbsp oil, 5 eggs, salt, 200 g flour, $^1/_2$ tsp baking powder, 300 g potatoes cooked in their skins, 300 g porcini mushrooms, 1 onion, 200 g butter, pepper, $^1/_2$ tsp ground nutmeg, $^1/_2$ tsp ground coriander, fat for greasing

1 Pre-heat the oven to 220 °C (Gas Mark 7). Mix together the quark, milk, oil, 1 egg and a little salt. Mix the flour and baking powder and stir into the quark mixture to give an elastic dough. Transfer the dough to a greased springform tin (26 cm diameter) and press firmly around the edges.

2 Peel the potatoes and cut in slices. Trim the mushrooms, wipe with a damp cloth and cut in slices. Peel and dice the onion.

3 Heat 50 g butter in a pan and brown the onion lightly. Add the sliced mushrooms and after 3 minutes add the sliced potatoes. Flavour to taste with salt, pepper, nutmeg and coriander.

4 Spoon the mushroom and potato mixture onto the dough and bake in the oven for about 25 minutes. Heat the remaining butter until it is clear, then leave to cool. Separate the remaining eggs. Mix the clarified butter with the egg yolks. Pour over the cake and bake in the oven for a further 5 minutes. Serve hot.

Preparation time: approx. 35 minutes (plus approx. 30 minutes baking time)
Per serving approx. 251 kcal/1054 kJ; 8 g P, 17 g F, 17 g CH

Potato cakes

Serves 4

1 kg potatoes, salt, 200 g smoked sausage, 2 garlic cloves, 1 shallot, 1 egg, pepper, $^1/_2$ tsp dried marjoram, 100 g flour, 2 tbsp freshly chopped parsley, 150 g clarified butter

1   Wash the potatoes and in boil a little salted water for about 25 minutes. Then drain, let the remaining water evaporate, peel while still hot and mash with a fork.

2   Cut the sausage in very small cubes. Peel the garlic cloves and the shallot and chop finely. Work the mashed potato, sausage and the other ingredients except for the fat into a dough.

3   Melt the clarified butter in a pan. Using your hands, form the dough into small, flat cakes and fry in the butter. Drain on kitchen roll. Serve with a green salad.

Preparation time: approx. 15 minutes (plus approx. 25 minutes cooking time and approx. 10 minutes for frying)
Per portion approx. 530 kcal/2226 kJ; 11 g P, 28 g F, 56 g CH

Bacon dumplings

Serves 4

6 stale bread rolls, 250 ml milk, 250 g pork belly, 3 tbsp freshly chopped chives,
3 eggs, 3 tbsp flour, salt, pepper

1 Cut the rolls into small cubes and soak in warmed milk for 10 minutes. Dice the bacon and render in a pan until crisp. Drain on kitchen roll.

2 Squeeze the liquid out of the rolls and mix with the bacon, chives, eggs and flour. If necessary, add a little milk. Season with salt and pepper and leave to rest for 20 minutes.

3 Bring a pan of salted water to the boil. Moisten your hands and form the mixture into dumplings. Cook in the boiling water until they rise to the surface. Drain and serve with salad.

Preparation time: approx. 20 minutes (plus approx. 10 minutes for soaking,
approx. 20 minutes resting time and approx. 10 minutes cooking time)
Per portion approx. 807 kcal/3389 kJ; 15 g P, 63 g F, 44 g CH

Bulgur kibbeh

Serves 4

250 g bulgur wheat, 2 medium aubergines, 2 garlic cloves, $^1/_2$ red chilli, 1 tsp cornflour, 1 large onion, $^1/_2$ tsp ground allspice, $^1/_2$ tsp ground coriander, salt, sunflower oil for frying, 1 bunch parsley

1 Tip the bulgur into a bowl, just cover with water and soak for approx. 20 minutes. Wash and trim the aubergines and chop coarsely. Peel the garlic and chop coarsely. Trim, wash and dry the chilli.

2 Pour the bulgur into a sieve, drain and transfer to a bowl. Purée the aubergines, garlic and chilli in a blender and add to the bulgur. Mix the cornflour with a little water and add to the mixture. Peel the onion, chop and add to the mixture with the spices and a little salt. Knead the mixture well, form into little balls and press slightly flat.

3 Heat the oil in a pan and fry the kibbeh over medium heat until golden brown. Leave to drain on kitchen roll. Wash the parsley, shake dry and chop. Sprinkle the kibbeh with parsley and serve.

Preparation time: approx. 20 minutes (plus approx. 20 minutes for soaking and approx. 10 minutes for frying)
Per portion approx. 578 kcal/2426 kJ; 40 g P, 5 g F, 93 g CH

Bulgur and lentil rissoles

Serves 4

100 g red lentils, 100 g bulgur wheat,
8 dried tomatoes, $^1/_2$ bunch flat-leaf parsley,
200 g feta, 2 eggs, 50 g flour, $^1/_2$ tsp salt,
pepper, $^1/_2$ tsp cumin, 4 tbsp olive oil

1 Bring the lentils to the boil in about
200 ml water and simmer over low heat for
approx. 10 minutes. Tip the bulgur into a
bowl and cover with boiling water to about
2 cm above the bulgur. Leave to swell. Pour
hot water over the dried tomatoes and leave
to swell.

2 Wash the parsley and pat dry. Chop
the leaves finely. Drain the feta and cut in
cubes. Remove the tomatoes from the water,
pat dry and dice.

3 Tip the lentils and bulgur into a sieve and
drain. Transfer to a bowl. Add the parsley,
feta and tomatoes. Mix in the eggs and
flour. Season well with salt, pepper and
cumin.

4 Heat half the oil in a nonstick pan. Form
flat rissoles from the mixture and panfry
on both sides, a portion at a time, for about
5 minutes. Keep the finished rissoles warm
in the oven at a very low setting and fry
more rissoles in the remaining oil.

Preparation time: approx. 30 minutes (plus approx. 10 minutes to swell
and approx. 20 minutes for frying)
Per portion approx. 460 kcal/1920 kJ; 22 g P, 23 g F, 40 g CH

Carrot pancakes

with herb quark

Serves 4

2 onions, 500 g carrots, 200 g potatoes, 40 g Gruyère cheese, 30 g pumpkin seeds,
2 eggs, 50 g flour, salt, pepper, $1/2$ tsp ground coriander, $1/2$ tsp curry powder,
3 tbsp clarified butter, 250 g quark, 150 g yoghurt, $1/2$ tsp mustard, $1/2$ tsp ground
paprika, 1 pinch cayenne pepper, 6 tbsp freshly chopped herbs, shoots for garnishing

1 Peel the onions. Wash, peel and trim the carrots and potatoes. Shred all these with a vegetable grater and tip into a bowl. Grate the Gruyère and chop the pumpkin seeds. Mix these with the eggs, flour, salt, pepper and herbs.

2 Form round pancakes from the mixture and fry in hot clarified butter until crisp.

3 For the dip, mix together the quark, yoghurt, mustard, paprika, cayenne pepper and herbs. Season with salt and pepper and serve with the pancakes.

Preparation time: approx. 20 minutes (plus approx. 10 minutes for frying)
Per portion approx. 327 kcal/1373 kJ; 24 g P, 12 g F, 27 g CH

Rich in vitamins

Frankfurter and vegetable skewers

Serves 4

6 frankfurters, 2 courgettes, 1 red and 1 yellow pepper, 2 onions, 1 garlic clove, 3 tbsp olive oil, salt, pepper, sweet paprika powder

1 Cut the frankfurters in pieces approx. 3 cm long. Wash, dry and trim the courgettes and cut in half lengthways, then in slices approx. 2 cm thick. Trim the peppers, wash and dry inside and out and cut in pieces of approx. 2 cm. Peel the onion and cut in eight. Spear pieces of frankfurter and vegetable alternately on 8 metal skewers.

2 Crush the garlic clove in a press and mix with the olive oil. Mix in the salt, pepper and a little paprika and baste the skewers with this. Panfry on all sides for approx. 10 minutes.

Preparation time: approx. 20 minutes (plus approx. 10 minutes for frying)
Per portion approx. 191 kcal/802 kJ; 8 g P, 16 g F, 2 g CH

Malfatti

Serves 4

700 g leaf spinach, salt, 150 g ricotta or other cream cheese, 3 egg yolks, 60 g flour, pepper, ground nutmeg, 3 tbsp butter, 60 g Parmesan, fat for greasing

For little Popeyes!

1 Trim the spinach, wash thoroughly, transfer still wet to a pan and wilt over medium heat, stirring continuously. Remove from the pan, drain in a colander and squeeze out the moisture. Then chop finely.

2 In a bowl, mix together the ricotta, egg yolks and flour until smooth. Fold in the spinach and mix to a smooth dough. Season to taste with salt, pepper and nutmeg.

3 Bring salted water to the boil in a large pan. With a spoon, scoop small dumplings out of the spinach mixture and drop them into the water. Simmer over medium heat for about 10 minutes until they rise to the surface.

4 Fish the dumplings out of the water, drain and transfer to a greased ovenproof dish. Top with flakes of butter and freshly grated Parmesan. Gratinate under a hot grill for about 3 minutes. Serve with tomato salad.

Preparation time: approx. 30 minutes (plus approx. 10 minutes cooking time and approx. 10 minutes to gratinate)
Per portion approx. 535 kcal/2247 kJ; 18 g P, 45 g F, 13 g CH

Courgette and ham frittata

Serves 4

4 tbsp olive oil, 400 g courgettes, 2 onions, 120 g cooked ham, 12 eggs, salt, pepper, 300 g yoghurt, 2 tsp finely chopped chives

1 Heat the olive oil in a pan. Wash and trim the courgettes and peel the onions. Slice both thinly and fry briefly until transparent. Cut the ham into thin strips. Add to the courgettes and onions and brown briefly.

2 Beat the eggs and season with salt and pepper. Pour over the vegetables and ham, cover and cook over low heat for approx. 8 minutes until firm.

3 Turn once and cook on the other side for a further 1–2 minutes without the lid. Leave to cool and cut into eight.

4 Mix the yoghurt with a little salt and a pinch of pepper, and sprinkle with chives. Transfer to a small bowl and serve with the frittata.

Fresh!

Preparation time: approx. 20 minutes (plus approx. 10 minutes for frying)
Per portion approx. 720 kcal/3014 kJ; 34 g P, 44 g F, 46 g CH

Dumpling roll

Serves 4

250 g stale bread rolls, 1 onion, 70 g butter, 3 eggs, 300 ml milk, salt, 150 g flour,
$^1/_2$ bunch flat-leaf parsley, butter for brushing

1 Dice the rolls. Peel the onion and dice finely. Heat the butter and sauté the diced onion until transparent. Beat the eggs with the milk and 1 teaspoon salt. Add the diced bread and onion and mix thoroughly with the flour. Wash the parsley, shake dry, chop the leaves and stir into the bread mixture. Leave to rest for about 30 minutes.

2 Tip the dough onto a tea towel brushed with butter and form into a roll about 6 cm in diameter. Wrap the dough in the cloth and tie up the ends with kitchen string. Place the roll in a pan of boiling salted water. Cook for about 40 minutes over medium heat.

3 Leave the dumpling roll to rest for 10 minutes, then unwrap it and cut in slices about 1 cm thick. Serve with salad.

Preparation time: approx. 30 minutes (plus approx. 30 minutes resting time and approx. 40 minutes cooking time)
Per portion approx. 535 kcal/2247 kJ; 17 g P, 23 g F, 63 g CH

Strammer Max

Serves 4

4 slices farmhouse bread, 70 g butter, 4 slices cooked ham, 4 eggs, salt, pepper, ¹/₂ bunch chives, 2 gherkins

Quick

1 Spread the slices of bread with a little butter. Top each one with a slice of ham.

2 Melt the remaining butter in a nonstick pan over medium heat and fry 4 eggs. Salt and pepper them. Place a fried egg on each slice of bread.

3 Wash the chives, shake dry and cut in rounds. Slice the gherkins. Sprinkle with chives and serve with the gherkins.

Preparation time: approx. 10 minutes (plus approx. 10 minutes frying time)
Per portion approx. 350 kcal/1470 kJ; 16 g P, 21 g F, 21 g CH

Bacon pancakes
with lamb's lettuce

Serves 4

For the bacon pancakes: 8 eggs, approx. 200 g flour, 200 ml milk, mineral water, salt, pepper, 250 g streaky bacon, 4 tbsp clarified butter; for the salad: 1 $1/_2$ tsp mustard, 3 tbsp apple vinegar, salt, pepper, 4–5 tbsp sunflower oil, 1 pinch sugar, 200 g lamb's lettuce

1 Separate the eggs. Mix the yolks with the flour and milk and add enough mineral water to give a fluid batter. Beat the egg whites until stiff and mix into the batter a portion at a time. Season with salt and pepper.

2 Cut the bacon in small cubes and reduce in a pan. Reserve 1 tablespoon diced bacon and the bacon fat and mix the remaining bacon into the batter. For each of 4 pancakes, heat 1 tablespoon clarified butter, fry one at a time and keep warm.

3 Make a dressing from mustard, vinegar, salt, pepper, bacon fat, sunflower oil and sugar. Pull the lamb's lettuce apart, trim, wash and shake dry. Transfer to a bowl and pour over the dressing. Sprinkle the remaining bacon over the salad. Serve the pancakes with the lamb's lettuce salad.

Preparation time: approx. 20 minutes (plus approx. 20 minutes cooking time)
Per portion approx. 522 kcal/2192 kJ; 33 g P, 25 g F, 39 g CH

Sausage salad
with mountain cheese

Serves 4

400 g Bologna sausage, 100 g strong-flavoured mountain cheese, 2 gherkins, 1 bunch spring onions, 1 bunch chives, 6 tbsp apple vinegar, 2 tsp medium-hot mustard, sugar, salt, pepper, 6 tbsp vegetable oil, 1 small onion in rings, 2 tbsp chopped parsley

1 Skin the sausage and cut in thin strips. Cut off the cheese rind and cut the cheese in thin strips also. Dice the gherkins.

2 Trim, wash and dry the spring onions and cut in thin rings. Wash the chives, pat dry and cut in small rounds. Mix together the vinegar and mustard and flavour with sugar, salt and pepper. Then mix in the oil.

3 Mix together the sausage and cheese, pour over the dressing, mix well and leave to draw for at least 30 minutes.

4 Fold the gherkins and spring onions into the salad and serve sprinkled with onion rings and parsley.

Preparation time: approx. 20 minutes (plus approx. 30 minutes to draw)
Per portion approx. 410 kcal/1722 kJ; 22 g P, 34 g F, 3 g CH

Hot grapes
with almond crumble

Serves 4

800 g seedless grapes (white or red), 125 g sugar, 125 ml grape juice, juice of $1/2$ lemon, 125 g flour, $1/2$ tsp baking powder, 1 pinch ground cinnamon, 50 g crème fraîche, 1 drop bitter almond oil, 50 g chopped almonds, 60 g cold butter, icing sugar for dusting, cream or vanilla ice cream as desired

1 Pre-heat the oven to 180 °C (Gas Mark 4). Wash the grapes, pat dry, remove the stalks and spread out on a baking sheet. Sprinkle the grapes with 25 g sugar, pour over the grape juice and lemon juice and bake on the middle shelf of the oven for 5 minutes.

2 Mix together the flour, baking powder, the remaining sugar and cinnamon and tip into a bowl. Add the crème fraîche and bitter almond oil. Knead with the almonds and butter to a crumble. Remove the grapes from the oven, transfer to 4 individual ovenproof dishes and spread the crumble evenly over the grapes.

3 Return to the oven and bake for approx. 25 minutes until golden brown. Dust with icing sugar. Best served lukewarm with whipped cream or vanilla ice cream.

Preparation time: approx. 20 minutes (plus approx. 30 minutes baking time)
Per portion approx. 580 kcal/2436 kJ; 7 g P, 18 g F, 94 g CH

Rice pudding
with rhubarb and strawberry compote

Serves 4

For the rice pudding: 1 litre milk, 1 pinch salt, 100 g sugar, 250 g pudding rice, 1 tsp ground cinnamon; for the rhubarb and strawberry compote: 500 g rhubarb, 1 vanilla pod, 4 tbsp orange juice, 4 tbsp sugar, 500 g strawberries

1 In a pan bring the milk to the boil with the salt and 75 g sugar. Stir in the rice and simmer for about 30 minutes, stirring regularly.

2 For the compote, wash, trim and peel the rhubarb and cut in bite-size pieces. Cut open the vanilla pod and scrape out the pith. In a pan, gently stew the rhubarb with the vanilla pith, orange juice and sugar for about 10 minutes. Trim and wash the strawberries and cut in half. Mix the rhubarb with the strawberries.

3 Spoon the rice into a serving bowl. Mix the remaining sugar with the cinnamon and sprinkle over the rice pudding. Serve with the rhubarb and strawberry compote.

Preparation time: approx. 25 minutes (plus approx. 30 minutes cooking time)
Per portion approx. 345 kcal/1449 kJ; 10 g P, 10 g F, 51 g CH

Deep-fried apple rings

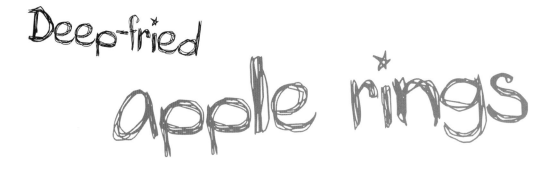

Serves 4

1 tsp dried yeast, 50 g flour, 50 g butter, 125 ml milk, 3 eggs, 25 g sugar, 8 apples, vegetable oil for frying, icing sugar for dusting

Simply delicious!

1 Dissolve the dried yeast in 3 tablespoons of warm water. Make a smooth yeast batter from the flour, yeast, butter, milk, eggs and sugar. Cover and leave to rise for approx. 20 minutes.

2 Peel and core the apples and cut in rings. Coat the apple rings in the batter and deep fry in hot vegetable oil until golden brown. Dust with icing sugar.

Preparation time: approx. 15 minutes (plus approx. 20 minutes to rise and approx. 10 minutes for frying)
Per portion approx. 405 kcal/1696 kJ; 9 g P, 20 g F, 46 g CH

Cherry and poppy seed soufflé

Serves 4

150 ml milk, $1/2$ packet vanilla sauce powder, 150 g rusk, 1 jar Morello cherries (350 g), 3 eggs, 100 g sugar, 1 packet vanilla sugar, 1 packet poppy seed filling (250 g), 500 g low-fat quark, 4 tbsp flour, 1 packet baking powder, fat for greasing, 50 g flaked almonds, icing sugar for dusting

1 Pre-heat the oven to 175 °C (Gas Mark 4). Heat the milk, add the vanilla sauce powder, mix well and soak 100 g rusk in it. Crumble the remaining 50 g finely and set aside. Drain the cherries. Separate the eggs and beat the whites stiff. Mix the yolks with the sugar, vanilla sugar and poppy seed filling.

2 Squeeze a little of the liquid out of the soaked rusk and mix with the quark. Mix together the flour and baking powder and fold into the rusk mixture. Carefully fold in the egg whites. Transfer half the mixture to a greased soufflé dish.

3 Cover with the cherries, then with the crumbled rusk. Top with the remaining poppy seed mixture and smooth over. Sprinkle with almond flakes and bake in the oven for 35–40 minutes. Dust with icing sugar and serve.

Preparation time: approx. 45 minutes
(plus approx. 40 minutes baking time)
Per portion approx. 535 kcal/2247 kJ; 24 g P, 15 g F, 73 g CH

Apples in blankets

Serves 4

1 packet frozen puff pastry (450 g), 4 apples, 1 tbsp raisins, sugar, cinnamon, 1 egg yolk, 2 tbsp cream, flour for the worktop

1 Thaw the pastry following the instructions on the packet and roll out slightly on a floured worktop. Cut the pastry in squares with sides of 15 cm.

2 Pre-heat the oven to 225 °C (Gas Mark 7). Peel and core the apples and place them on the squares of pastry. Fill the apples with the raisins, sprinkle with a little sugar and cinnamon and fold the pastry together over the apples.

3 Beat together the egg yolk and cream and brush the pastry with it. Place the apples on a baking sheet lined with parchment and bake in the oven for about 30 minutes. If desired, serve with whipped cream.

Preparation time: approx. 20 minutes (plus approx. 30 minutes baking time)
Per portion approx. 219 kcal/919 kJ; 2 g P, 11 g F, 26 g CH

Plum and ricotta pastries

> Makes a nice change

Makes 12

1 packet frozen puff pastry (450 g),
250 g ricotta, 50 g sugar, 40 g butter,
2 eggs, 150 g plums

1 Thaw the sheets of puff pastry. Pre-heat the oven to 225 °C (Gas Mark 7).

2 Cut the sheets of pastry in half and place them on a baking sheet lined with parchment. Beat the ricotta, sugar, butter and eggs until creamy. Spoon this cream onto the middle of the pastry sheets.

3 Wash the plums, pat dry, remove the stones and cut the flesh in segments. Top the cream with 3 segments on each pastry. Bake in the oven for about 20 minutes.

Preparation time: approx. 10 minutes
(plus approx. 20 minutes baking time)
Per pastry approx. 248 kcal/1044 kJ; 5 g P, 18 g F, 16 g CH

Main dishes

In these recipes even the vegetables are tasty. Delicious soufflés, favourite classics, healthy fish dishes and much more offer a wide selection of great dishes that will make children and grown-ups equally happy. We have also included some substantial sweet dishes here.

Vegetable and egg bake

Serves 4

6–8 eggs, salt, pepper, 1 tbsp finely chopped parsley, 2 carrots, 3 parsnips,
3 tbsp walnut oil, 200 g sweet potatoes, 1 pinch each of fennel seeds, powdered cloves,
cinnamon, cardamom and powdered star anise, fat for greasing

1 Pre-heat the oven to 170 °C (Gas Mark 3.5). Break the eggs into a bowl, season with salt and pepper and beat together with the parsley. Trim, wash and peel the carrots and parsnips and cut in thin slices.

2 Heat the oil and fry the sliced vegetables for approx. 8 minutes. Wash, peel and dice the sweet potatoes and add to the pan with the other vegetables. Season well with the spices.

3 Transfer the vegetables to a greased shallow ovenproof dish and pour over the egg mixture. Bake on the middle shelf of the oven for approx. 40 minutes. Cut in pieces and serve. Asian plum sauce goes well with this.

Aromatic

Preparation time: approx. 30 minutes (plus approx. 40 minutes cooking time)
Per portion approx. 369 kcal/1549 kJ; 18 g P, 21 g F, 17 g CH

Ratatouille lasagne

Serves 4

3 small peppers (red, yellow, green), $^1/_2$ courgette, 1 onion, $^1/_2$ aubergine, 2 tomatoes, 3 tbsp walnut oil, 2 tbsp finely chopped French herbs (e.g. thyme, rosemary, savoury or marjoram), 20 ml fruit vinegar, 200 ml vegetable stock, salt, pepper, 250 g lasagne sheets, 200 g blue-veined cheese, 50 g butter flakes, 50 g breadcrumbs, fat for greasing

1 Wash, trim and dice the vegetables, then fry in hot walnut oil for approx. 4 minutes. Add the herbs, fruit vinegar and stock and cook for a further 5–6 minutes. Season with salt and pepper.

2 Grease an ovenproof dish. Pre-heat the oven to 180 °C (Gas Mark 4). Arrange a layer of lasagne sheets on the bottom of the dish.

3 Add alternate layers of vegetables and lasagne, with the last layer of vegetables. Crumble the blue-veined cheese over it.

4 Mix the butter flakes with the breadcrumbs and top the vegetables with it. Bake on the middle shelf of the oven for approx. 35 minutes. Remove from the oven and serve.

Preparation time: approx. 30 minutes (plus approx. 35 minutes baking time)
Per portion approx. 517 kcal/2171 kJ; 16 g P, 19 g F, 66 g CH

Broccoli bake

Serves 4

500 g broccoli, 2 red peppers, salt, 400 g gnocchi, 30 g herb butter, 30 g wheat flour, 250 ml milk, 3 tbsp cream, pepper, coriander powder, 120 g grated medium mature Gouda, butter for greasing

1 Trim and wash the broccoli and cut in rosettes. Trim and wash the peppers, pat dry and cut in strips. Blanch the broccoli in lightly salted water for approx. 6 minutes, then drain and rinse in cold water. Cook the gnocchi in boiling lightly salted water until they rise to the surface, then drain.

2 Pre-heat the oven to 180 °C (Gas Mark 4). Heat the herb butter in a pan and stir in the flour. Add the milk and cream, mix thoroughly and season with salt, pepper and coriander powder. Bring to the boil, stirring continuously.

3 Mix in the cheese and let it melt. Grease an ovenproof dish with butter and fill with alternate layers of vegetables and gnocchi. Spread the sauce over the top and bake on the middle shelf of the oven for approx. 15 minutes.

Preparation time: approx. 30 minutes (plus approx. 6 minutes for blanching and approx. 15 minutes for baking)
Per portion approx. 580 kcal/2436 kJ; 27 g P, 22 g F, 76 g CH

Penne
with fennel cream

Serves 4

200 g penne, salt, 2 fennel bulbs, 200 g sweet potatoes, 3–4 tbsp olive oil, pepper, powdered anise, cloves and allspice, 500 ml vegetable stock, 4–5 tbsp sour cream, 100 g strong-flavoured, grated hard cheese, fat for greasing

1   Cook the pasta in plenty of salted water following the instructions on the packet. Trim and wash the fennel bulbs and chop finely, including the green parts. Wash, trim and peel the sweet potatoes, and dice.

2   Heat the oil and cook the vegetables for approx. 10 minutes. Crush with a fork and season well with the spices. Add the vegetable stock and simmer over low heat for approx. 3 minutes. Mix in the sour cream.

3   Pre-heat the oven to 220 °C (Gas Mark 7). Grease a shallow ovenproof dish. Transfer the pasta to the dish and pour over the fennel cream. Sprinkle with the cheese and bake on the top shelf of the oven for approx. 6 minutes until golden brown.

Preparation time: approx. 30 minutes (plus approx. 6 minutes to gratinate)
Per portion approx. 703 kcal/2955 kJ; 17 g P, 46 g F, 49 g CH

Macaroni cheese

Serves 4

500 g macaroni, salt, 140 g Emmental cheese, 60 g Parmesan, 6 onions, 8 tbsp oil, 20 g butter

1 Cook the macaroni al dente in plenty of salted water following the instructions on the packet. Grate both kinds of cheese and mix together. Peel the onions and cut in rings.

2 Fill an ovenproof dish with alternate layers of macaroni and cheese, finishing with a layer of cheese. Bake in a pre-heated oven at 180 °C (Gas Mark 4) for approx. 15 minutes.

3 Fry the onions in hot oil. Add the butter and continue frying. Then drain on kitchen roll and arrange on the macaroni.

Preparation time: approx. 15 minutes (plus approx. 10 minutes cooking time and approx. 15 minutes baking time)
Per portion approx. 785 kcal/3285 kJ; 31 g P, 34 g F, 89 g CH

Gnocchi
alla piemontese

Serves 4

800 g floury potatoes, salt, 800 g tomatoes, 1 bunch sage, 1 onion, 1 garlic clove, 3 tbsp olive oil, pepper, 200 g flour, 2 tbsp butter, 100 g Parmesan

1 Wash the potatoes and put in a pan. Cover with water and $^1/_4$ teaspoon of salt and cook over low heat for approx. 20 minutes. Drain the potatoes, allow to cool briefly and peel.

2 Meanwhile cut a cross in the tomatoes and plunge in boiling water. Then rinse in cold water, peel, cut in four and remove the seeds and stalk ends. Dice the flesh. Wash the sage, pat dry and pick off the leaves.

3 Peel the onion and garlic and chop very finely. Heat the olive oil in a pan and fry the onion and garlic until transparent. Then add the diced tomatoes and reduce over low heat. Season well with salt and pepper.

4 Squeeze the potatoes through a ricer while still hot and season with a little salt. Knead the flour into the mashed potato to give a smooth dough. As soon as it no longer sticks to your hands add no more flour. Form portions of dough into small rolls about 2 cm in diameter and cut these in pieces 3 cm long.

5 In a large pan, bring 2 litres of water to the boil with $^1/_2$ teaspoon of salt. As soon as the water boils, add the gnocchi using a slotted spoon and reduce the heat. Let the gnocchi simmer for 4–5 minutes without the lid. As soon as they float to the surface of the water, scoop them out with the slotted spoon and leave to drain.

6 Melt the butter in a pan and briefly fry the sage leaves. Add the gnocchi and shake well. Serve with the tomato sauce and sprinkle with plenty of freshly grated Parmesan.

Preparation time: approx. 30 minutes (plus approx. 20 minutes cooking time)
Per portion approx. 560 kcal/2340 kJ; 19 g P, 21 g F, 71 g CH

Liver dumpling soup with chives

Serves 4

5 stale bread rolls, 250 ml milk, 2 eggs, 250 g calf's liver, salt, pepper, 1 tsp freshly chopped marjoram, 1 $\frac{1}{2}$ litres meat stock, 2 tbsp chives, in rings

1 Cut the rolls into small cubes. Heat the milk and pour over the cubes of bread. Cover and leave to soak for about 30 minutes.

2 Break the eggs into a bowl. Wash the liver, pat dry, remove the skin and sinews and chop finely or run through a mincer. Season with salt, pepper and marjoram and add to the eggs. Add the bread cubes and work into a smooth dough.

3 Heat the stock in a pan. Moisten your hands, form fist-sized liver dumplings and simmer in the stock for about 20 minutes. Serve sprinkled with chive rings.

Preparation time: approx. 20 minutes (plus approx. 30 minutes to soak and approx. 20 minutes cooking time)
Per portion approx. 317 kcal/1331 kJ; 22 g P, 9 g F, 35 g CH

Warming

Chicken noodle soup

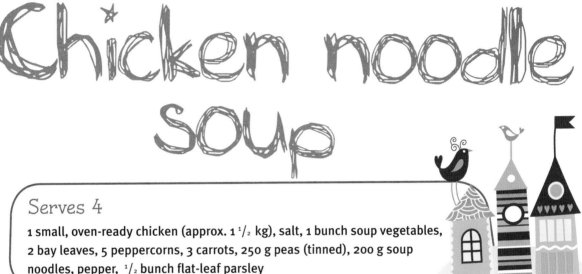

Serves 4

1 small, oven-ready chicken (approx. 1 $^1/_2$ kg), salt, 1 bunch soup vegetables, 2 bay leaves, 5 peppercorns, 3 carrots, 250 g peas (tinned), 200 g soup noodles, pepper, $^1/_2$ bunch flat-leaf parsley

1 Wash the chicken and put in a large pan. Cover with salted water. Bring to the boil and skim off the scum. Trim and wash the soup vegetables and peel and dice as required. Add the vegetables, bay leaves and peppercorns to the chicken and simmer gently for about 1 hour and 30 minutes.

2 Remove the chicken from the soup and leave to cool. Separate the meat from the skin and bones and cut in cubes. Strain the stock.

3 Trim and peel the carrots and cut in thin sticks. Drain the peas. Simmer the carrots in the soup for about 5 minutes, then add the peas and noodles and simmer for a further 5 minutes. Add the chopped chicken to the soup and season to taste with salt and pepper. Wash the parsley, shake dry and chop. Garnish the soup with parsley and serve.

Preparation time: approx. 30 minutes (plus approx. 1 hour 30 minutes cooking time)
Per portion approx. 882 kcal/3704 kJ; 58 g P, 52 g F, 43 g CH

Main dishes

Dumplings
with mushroom ragout

Serves 4

6 stale bread rolls, 200 ml lukewarm milk, salt, pepper, grated nutmeg, 4 shallots,
$^1/_2$ bunch flat-leaf parsley, 2 tbsp butter, 600 g fresh mushrooms, e.g. chanterelles,
porcini mushrooms or button mushrooms, 50 g streaky bacon, 2 eggs, 1–2 tbsp
breadcrumbs, 100 ml vegetable stock, 150 g crème fraîche

1 Cut the rolls into small cubes. Tip into a bowl, pour over the milk and season with salt,
pepper and a pinch of nutmeg. Leave to draw for approx. 20 minutes. Peel the shallots and
chop very finely. Wash the parsley, pat dry and chop the leaves finely. Melt 1 tablespoon of
butter in a pan and lightly brown half of the shallots. Add a teaspoon of parsley, fry briefly
and leave to cool.

2 Clean the mushrooms, i.e. wipe gently with kitchen roll and cut off the ends of the stalks.
Do not cut up chanterelles; if using porcini or button mushrooms, cut in slices. Dice the
bacon.

3 In a large pan bring 2 litres of salted water to the boil. Knead together the bread mixture,
the cooled shallots and the eggs and season to taste with salt, pepper and nutmeg. Form
the dough into 8–10 dumplings of equal size. If the dough is too moist and sticky, knead in
a small quantity of breadcrumbs. As soon as the water boils, carefully slip the dumplings in
with the aid of a slotted spoon and simmer over low heat for 15–20 minutes.

4 In the meantime, melt 1 tablespoon of butter in a pan. Brown the remaining shallots and
the diced bacon, then add the mushrooms, brown briefly and season with salt and pepper.
Add the stock, gently stir in the crème fraîche and simmer for 5 minutes over low heat.

5 Season the mushroom ragout once more to taste, then spoon onto plates, place the
dumplings on top, sprinkle with the remaining chopped parsley and serve immediately.

Preparation time: approx. 20 minutes (plus approx. 20 minutes to draw and 20 minutes cooking time)
Per portion approx. 580 kcal/ 2420 kJ; 18 g P, 35 g F, 44 g CH

Cheese spätzle

Serves 4

500 g wheat flour, 4 eggs, 1 tsp sea salt, 1 pinch nutmeg, pepper, 70 g butter, mineral water, 2 large onions, 400 g Emmental or mountain cheese

1 Pre-heat the oven to 80 °C (Gas Mark ⅙). Knead the flour, eggs, a pinch of salt, nutmeg, pepper and 50 g butter to a dough, then mix in just enough mineral water to make the spätzle dough elastic and develop bubbles. The spätzle dough should be viscous and drip slowly from the spoon. Leave the dough to rest for 15 minutes. Meanwhile peel the onions and cut in rings and grate the cheese.

2 Bring salted water to the boil, then reduce the heat so that the water is barely simmering. Squeeze the dough a portion at a time through a spätzle press into the water.

3 When the spätzle float to the surface, scoop them out with a slotted spoon and leave to drain. Then tip them into a bowl, sprinkle immediately with a little cheese, season with pepper and keep warm in the pre-heated oven. Then cook the next portion of spätzle and continue in this way until all the dough is used up. Sprinkle the last layer with the remaining with cheese.

4 Heat the remaining butter in a pan over low heat and fry the onion rings until golden brown. Remove the cheese spätzle from the oven, garnish with the onions and serve. A mixed or green salad goes well with this.

Preparation time: approx. 35 minutes (plus approx. 15 minutes resting time
and approx. 15 minutes cooking time)
Per portion approx. 577 kcal/2423 kJ; 37 g P, 47 g F, 2 g CH

Coley fillet
with potato salad

Serves 4

For the potato salad: 750 g potatoes, 1 cucumber, salt, pepper, 5 tbsp apple vinegar, 5 tbsp oil, 2 tbsp chopped dill; for the fish: 4 coley fillets, salt, pepper, 6 tbsp flour, 1 egg, 50 g breadcrumbs, fat for frying

1 For the salad, boil the potatoes with the skin on and leave to cool.

2 Meanwhile, trim and peel the cucumber, cut in slices or shave, sprinkle with salt and leave to draw.

Healthy

3 Peel the potatoes and cut in slices. Put in a bowl and mix with salt, pepper, vinegar and oil.

4 Drain the cucumber and mix into the salad. Sprinkle with dill and leave the salad to draw for 20 minutes.

5 Wash the fish, pat dry and rub with salt and pepper. Toss the fillets in flour, beaten egg and breadcrumbs.

6 Heat plenty of fat. Fry the fillets on each side for approx. 3 minutes. Leave to drain on kitchen roll. Serve with the salad.

Preparation time: approx. 30 minutes (plus approx. 20 minutes cooking time and approx. 20 minutes for cooling)
Per portion approx. 435 kcal/1827 kJ; 40 g P, 10 g F, 43 g CH

Fish fillets

with a herb crust

Serves 4

4 medium mushrooms, 4 shallots, ¹/₂ bunch each of flat-leaf parsley, basil and chives, 100 g butter, 40 g breadcrumbs, yolk of 1 hard-boiled egg, 4 fish fillets (each about 150 g), salt, pepper, 100 ml vegetable stock, 1 tbsp lemon juice, fat for greasing

1 Trim the mushrooms, wipe with a damp cloth if necessary and chop finely. Peel the shallots and dice finely. Wash the parsley and basil, pat dry and pick the leaves off the stems. Reserve a few leaves of parsley for garnishing. Pre-heat the oven to 225 °C (Gas Mark 7).

2 Chop the remaining parsley and the basil and cut the chives in thin rounds. Knead together all the prepared herbs and vegetables with softened butter, breadcrumbs and the crushed egg yolk.

3 Wash the fish, pat dry and season with salt and pepper. Place skin side down in a greased ovenproof dish. Spread the mushroom and herb mixture evenly over the fish.

4 Add the stock and lemon juice and bake the fish in the pre-heated oven for approx. 12 minutes. Garnish with the parsley.

Preparation time: approx. 30 minutes
(plus approx. 12 minutes cooking time)
Per portion approx. 393 kcal/1649 kJ; 32 g P, 26 g F, 10 g CH

Dorado on red lentils

Serves 4

150 g red lentils, 2 shallots, 1 large carrot, ¹/₂ leek, 30 g butter, 1 bay leaf,
200 ml strong vegetable stock, 600 g dorado fillet, 100 g streaky bacon slices,
2 tbsp olive oil, sea salt, pepper, 2 sprigs thyme, 1 tsp lemon juice, 100 ml cream

1 Tip the lentils into a sieve, rinse and leave to drain. Peel and dice the shallots.
Wash and peel the carrot, wash and trim the leek and cut both in small cubes.

2 Heat 1 tablespoon of butter, add the shallots and fry briefly. Add the lentils,
bay leaf, vegetables and stock, bring to the boil and simmer over low heat for
10 minutes.

3 Rinse the fish in cold water, pat dry and cut in pieces. Cut the bacon slices in
thin strips.

4 Heat the remaining butter and the oil in a pan and fry the fish for about
2 minutes on each side. Season with salt and pepper, remove from the pan and
keep warm.

5 Add the bacon to the fat remaining in the pan and fry until crisp. Wash the
thyme, shake dry and pick off the leaves. Shortly before serving, beat the cream
stiff and add to the lentils along with the thyme leaves.

6 Season to taste with sea salt, pepper and a little lemon juice. Serve the lentils
and dorado together and pour over the bacon and fat.

Preparation time: approx. 20 minutes (plus approx. 10 minutes cooking time
and approx. 4 minutes frying time)
Per portion approx. 580 kcal/2420 kJ; 18 g P, 35 g F, 44 g CH

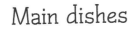
Salmon and macaroni nests

Serves 4

20 g pine nuts, 1 bunch basil, 1 garlic clove, 30 g freshly grated Parmesan, 3 tbsp fish stock or bouillon, 200 g mushrooms, 1 tbsp olive oil, 1 small onion, chopped, 4 tbsp bouillon, salt, pepper, 300 g salmon fillet, 1 lemon, 500 g macaroni, cooked and rinsed under cold water, 200 g mozzarella, diced, fat for greasing

1 Toast the pine nuts lightly in a dry pan. Wash the basil, shake dry and pick off the leaves. Peel the garlic and purée with the Parmesan, basil, pine nuts and fish stock in a rotary food chopper or with a hand blender.

2 Trim the mushrooms, wipe with a damp cloth and cut in slices. Peel and chop the onion. Brown the mushrooms and onion in hot oil. Add the bouillon and season with salt and pepper.

3 Pre-heat the oven to 180 °C (Gas Mark 4). Rinse the salmon, pat dry and cut in cubes of about 2 cm. Drizzle with lemon juice and season with salt.

4 Mix the basil paste into the macaroni. Wind the macaroni into strings and form nests on a greased baking sheet. Mix the salmon and mushrooms together and spoon into the nests. Top the nests with mozzarella and bake for approx. 30 minutes.

Preparation time: approx. 30 minutes (plus approx. 30 minutes baking time)
Per portion approx. 807 kcal/3390 kJ; 41 g P, 32 g F, 88 g CH

Potato and salmon quiche

Serves 4

2 potatoes (approx. 400 g), 250 g broccoli, salt, 100 g cave-matured cheese, 350 g low-fat quark, 3 eggs, 1–2 tsp mustard, 3 sprigs rosemary, 150 g hot-smoked salmon, diced, 1 tsp oregano, 4 tsp rapeseed oil, pepper, 2 rectangular sheets yufka/filo pastry (160 g), fat for greasing

1 Wash the potatoes and parboil for approx. 20 minutes. Then drain and let the remaining water evaporate. Trim and wash the broccoli, divide into florets and peel and dice the stems. Blanch in boiling salted water for approx. 2 minutes. Drain, rinse in cold water and leave to drip. Pre-heat the oven to 200 °C (Gas Mark 6).

2 Grate the cheese and mix with the quark, eggs and mustard. Peel and dice the potatoes. Wash the rosemary, pat dry and chop the leaves finely. Mix the quark cream together with the diced potato and salmon, the herbs, salt and 2 teaspoons of oil and season to taste with pepper.

3 Mix the remaining oil with 1 tablespoon of water. Brush the pastry sheets with this

and place them one on top of the other in a greased quiche tin (28 cm diameter). Add the filling and smooth over the top. Brush with remaining oil-and-water mixture and bake for approx. 35 minutes.

Preparation time: approx. 25 minutes (plus approx. 20 minutes cooking time and approx. 35 minutes baking time)
Per portion approx. 446 kcal/1872 kJ; 32 g P, 22 g F, 30 g CH

Salmon lasagne

Serves 4

300 g lasagne sheets, salt, 300 g salmon fillet, 3 tbsp lemon juice, 3 tbsp butter, 1 onion, diced, 1 garlic clove, chopped, 100 ml bouillon, 250 ml cream, pepper, grated rind of $^1/_2$ lemon, 100 g Gorgonzola, 100 g Pecorino, 50 g butter flakes for sprinkling, herbs for garnishing, butter for greasing

1 Cook the lasagne sheets al dente in boiling salted water for approx. 10 minutes. Wash the salmon, pat dry, drizzle with 2 tablespoons of lemon juice and season with salt. Then cut in cubes.

2 Heat the butter in a pan and sauté the onions and garlic. Then add the fish, bouillon and remaining lemon juice. Stir in the cream, reduce briefly and season with salt and pepper. Pre-heat the oven to 250 °C (Gas Mark 9).

3 Mix the lemon rind into the sauce. Crush the Gorgonzola with a fork and shave the Pecorino. Drain the lasagne.

4 Grease an ovenproof dish with butter and fill with alternate layers of pasta and salmon, finishing with a layer of pasta.

5 Top with the cheese and flakes of butter. Bake on the middle shelf of the oven for approx. 15 minutes. Garnish with herbs and serve.

Preparation time: approx. 30 minutes (plus approx. 15 minutes baking time)
Per portion approx. 948 kcal/3981 kJ; 37 g P, 63 g F, 41 g CH

Ham and cabbage fleckerl

Serves 4

Salt, 600 g ribbon noodles, 400 g cooked ham, 1 garlic clove, 4 eggs, 250 ml cream, pepper, ¹/₂ tsp grated nutmeg, 50 g butter, 100 g breadcrumbs, 500 g white cabbage, 2 tbsp clarified butter, cumin, fat for greasing

1 In a pan, bring plenty of salted water to the boil and cook the noodles following the instructions on the packet. Drain the noodles.

2 Pre-heat the oven to 200 °C (Gas Mark 6). Transfer the pasta to a greased ovenproof dish.

3 Dice the ham, peel the garlic and chop finely. Mix both with the noodles. Beat the eggs with the cream, salt, pepper and nutmeg and pour over the noodles.

4 Bake in the oven for about 30 minutes in all. After 20 minutes top with flakes of butter and sprinkle with the breadcrumbs.

5 Trim and wash the cabbage, remove the stalk and cut the leaves in strips. Stew in a pan in hot clarified butter for 30 minutes. Season with salt, pepper and cumin. Serve with the fleckerl.

Preparation time: approx. 20 minutes (plus approx. 30 minutes cooking time)
Per portion approx. 1090 kcal/4578 kJ; 51 g P, 39 g F, 130 g CH

Beef Stroganoff

Serves 4

400 g fillet of beef, 150 g tomatoes, 100 g mushrooms, 3 shallots, 4 tbsp oil,
2 tsp mustard, 250 g crème fraîche, salt, pepper, 3 tbsp liquid from dill cucumbers,
1 dill-pickled cucumber

1 Wash the beef, pat dry and cut in thin strips. Plunge the tomatoes first in boiling water then in cold, remove the stalk ends, skin and seeds and chop the flesh. Trim the mushrooms, wipe with a damp cloth and cut in slices. Peel and chop the shallots.

2 Heat the oil in a stew pan and lightly brown the shallots. Add the meat and fry thoroughly while stirring. Add the tomatoes and mushrooms and stir in the mustard and crème fraîche. Season with salt and pepper and flavour with the dill-pickle juice.

3 Lastly, dice the cucumber finely and mix into the Beef Stroganoff. Serve with ribbon noodles.

Preparation time: approx. 30 minutes
(plus approx. 15 minutes cooking time)
Per portion approx. 367 kcal/1541 kJ; 24 g P, 28 g F, 4 g CH

Classic

Ham noodles
with a cheese crust

Serves 4

400 g macaroni, salt, 250 g cooked ham, 250 g Emmental cheese, 6 eggs, 200 g sour cream, pepper, nutmeg, fat for greasing

1 Cook the macaroni al dente in plenty of boiling salted water, then drain. Dice the ham finely and grate the cheese.

2 Pre-heat the oven to 180 °C (Gas Mark 4). Fill a greased ovenproof dish with alternate layers of noodles, diced ham and grated cheese. Beat the eggs together with the sour cream and season with salt, pepper and nutmeg.

3 Pour this mixture over the ham and noodles and bake in the oven for about 40 minutes until the cheese crust is golden brown.

Preparation time: approx. 15 minutes (plus approx. 10 minutes cooking time and approx. 40 minutes baking time)
Per portion approx. 867 kcal/3641 kJ; 55 g P, 39 g F, 71 g CH

Herb chicken

Serves 4

2 oven-ready chickens (each 1.2 kg), 2 tsp salt, 2 tsp sweet paprika powder, 1 kg tomatoes, 4 garlic cloves, $^1/_2$ bunch flat-leaf parsley, 2 sprigs rosemary, 10 sprigs basil, 8 sprigs sage, 10 sprigs thyme, juice and rind of 1 untreated lemon, 4 tbsp olive oil, pepper, 1 tsp sugar

1 Pre-heat the oven to 200 °C (Gas Mark 6). Wash the chickens thoroughly inside and out under cold running water and pat dry. Cut away the excess skin at the neck and tail openings with a kitchen knife. Rub the chickens well inside and out with salt and paprika. Place the chickens on a baking sheet and roast on the second shelf from the bottom for about 50 minutes.

2 Meanwhile, for the sauce, cut a cross in the tomatoes, plunge first in boiling water then in cold, and peel. Cut in four, remove the seeds and stalk ends, and dice. Peel the garlic cloves and chop finely. Wash the herbs and pat dry with kitchen roll. Pick off the leaves of the parsley and rosemary and chop finely. Pick off the leaves of the basil and sage and cut in fine strips. Strip the thyme leaves off the stalks.

3 Put 2 garlic cloves and all the herbs except the basil in a small bowl. Add the lemon rind and juice. Mix in 2 tablespoons of olive oil and season well with pepper. 20 minutes before the end of cooking time baste the chickens with the seasoned oil.

4 For the tomato sauce, heat the remaining olive oil in a nonstick pan. Add the diced tomatoes and the remaining garlic and heat for 3–5 minutes. Flavour with the basil strips, salt, pepper and sugar. Divide the chickens into portions and serve with the tomato sauce.

Preparation time: approx. 30 minutes (plus approx. 1 hour cooking time)
Per portion approx. 570 kcal/2380 kJ; 53 g P, 35 g F, 12 g CH

Roast chicken legs

Serves 4

Sea salt, 1 kg small waxy potatoes, 2 sprigs rosemary, 4 chicken leg portions, salt, pepper, 2 tsp sweet paprika powder, 4 small courgettes, 1 large red pepper, 250 g cherry tomatoes

1 Line a baking sheet with parchment and sprinkle with coarse sea salt. Scrub the potatoes clean and place them on the baking sheet. Wash the rosemary, pick off the leaves and sprinkle over the potatoes.

2 Separate the chicken legs at the joints. Mix 1 teaspoon of salt with pepper and paprika powder and rub into the chicken pieces. Place them on the baking sheet in between the potatoes and roast in the pre-heated oven at 200 °C (Gas Mark 6) for about 45 minutes.

3 Wash and trim the courgettes and cut in strips. Remove the seeds from the pepper, wash and cut in thin strips. Wash and dry the cherry tomatoes and prick a few holes in them.

4 After about 25 minutes add the vegetables to the potatoes and chicken on the baking sheet.

Makes a nice change

Preparation time: approx. 25 minutes (plus approx. 45 minutes roasting time)
Per portion 488 kcal/2050 kJ; approx. 36 g P, 18 g F, 43 g CH

Lentil soup
with sausages

Serves 4

300 g lentils, 1 onion, 1 leek, 2 carrots, $^1/_4$ celeriac, 2–3 soup bones, 1 tbsp
sunflower oil, 4 small pork sausages, 1 tsp lovage, 1 tsp dried marjoram,
1 tsp salt, pepper, 1 tbsp vinegar

1 Put the lentils in a pan, cover with approx. 500 ml water, cover and soak for
12 hours, then drain.

2 When soaking is finished, peel the onion and chop very finely. Cut the green
part and the root off the leek. Wash the leek and cut diagonally in strips.

3 Wash, trim and peel the carrots. Cut the carrots in half lengthways first and
then in slices. Trim and peel the celeriac and cut in small cubes. Rinse the bones in
cold water and pat dry with kitchen roll.

4 Heat the sunflower oil in a large pan and fry the onion until transparent. Add
the chopped vegetables and brown lightly. Then add the soup bones, lentils and
1 litre of water and bring to the boil. Now reduce the heat, cover and simmer for
approx. 1 hour over low heat. Meanwhile slice the sausages and add to the soup
after 30 minutes.

5 Wash the lovage, pat dry with kitchen roll and chop finely with a large kitchen
knife. Remove the bones from the soup. Flavour the soup with lovage, marjoram,
salt, pepper and vinegar.

Preparation time: approx. 30 minutes (plus approx. 12 hours for soaking and approx. 1 hour cooking time)
Per portion approx. 510 kcal/2130 kJ; 32 g P, 23 g F, 44 g CH

Macaroni carbonara

Classic

Serves 4

2 garlic cloves, 150 g sliced bacon, 400 g macaroni, salt, 3 eggs, 150 ml cream,
80 g Parmesan, pepper, grated nutmeg

1 Peel the garlic and chop very finely. Cut the bacon in small pieces and fry in a nonstick pan over low heat. As soon as the bacon is crisp, remove from the pan and drain on kitchen roll. Add the garlic to the bacon fat and brown briefly.

2 Cook the macaroni al dente in plenty of salted water for about 10 minutes following the instructions on the packet. Tip into a colander and leave to drain. Then add the macaroni and bacon to the pan and mix well.

3 In a bowl beat the eggs, cream and 40 g grated Parmesan to a foam using a hand whisk. Season the egg mixture well with salt, pepper and a little grated nutmeg and fold into the macaroni. Heat briefly in the pan, without allowing the mixture to begin to set. Season again to taste with salt, pepper and nutmeg and serve sprinkled with the remaining Parmesan.

Preparation time: approx. 30 minutes
(plus approx. 10 minutes cooking time)
Per portion approx. 890 kcal/3720 kJ; 27 g P, 53 g F, 77 g CH

Fusilli with Bolognese sauce

> ### Serves 4
>
> 1 onion, 2 garlic cloves, 1 carrot, 1 leek, 1 stick celery, 100 g streaky bacon,
> 3 tbsp olive oil, 350 g minced beef, 2 tbsp tomato paste, 1 tbsp flour, 300 ml meat
> stock, salt, pepper, grated nutmeg, 1 tbsp dried oregano, 400 g fusilli, 100 g grated
> Parmesan

1 Peel the onion and the garlic cloves and chop finely. Wash, trim and peel the carrot and dice small. Trim the leek and celery, wash thoroughly, dry and dice small. Dice the bacon.

2 Heat the olive oil in a pan. Render the bacon, add the onion and fry gently until transparent. Add the garlic and vegetables and brown briefly. Add the mince and fry until crumbly, stirring continuously. Then stir in the tomato paste.

3 Dust with the flour and add the meat stock. Season well with salt, pepper, nutmeg and oregano, cover and simmer over low heat for approx. 20 minutes until the sauce thickens.

4 Cook the fusilli al dente in boiling salted water following the instructions on the packet. Tip into a colander, drain thoroughly and mix with the sauce. Transfer to plates and serve sprinkled with Parmesan.

Preparation time: approx. 30 minutes (plus approx. 20 minutes cooking time)
Per portion approx. 580 kcal/2420 kJ; 41 g P, 49 g F, 84 g CH

Ribbon noodles
with beef

Sophisticated

Serves 4

100 g walnuts, 750 g leeks, 500 g fillet of beef, 250 g mascarpone, salt, 3 tbsp balsamic vinegar, 2 egg yolks, 4 tbsp oil, white pepper, 500 g broad ribbon noodles

1 Chop the walnuts coarsely. Trim and wash the leeks and cut the white and pale green parts in rings approx. $^1/_2$ cm wide. Wash and dry the beef and cut first in slices $^1/_2$ cm thick and then in strips.

2 For the sauce, put the mascarpone in a pan. Mix in the salt and balsamic vinegar with a hand whisk. Heat the mixture and beat in the egg yolks, heating the sauce gently but not letting it boil, so that the egg binds it without setting.

3 Divide the oil between two pans and heat. In one pan, fry the strips of beef very fiercely a portion at a time for 1–2 minutes. In the second pan, lightly brown the leeks for 4–5 minutes, turning occasionally, then mix in the walnuts. Season the meat and leeks with salt and pepper.

4 Cook the noodles al dente in plenty of boiling salted water following the instructions on the packet, then leave to drain. Mix the noodles with the leek and strips of beef and pour over the mascarpone sauce.

Preparation time: approx. 30 minutes (plus approx. 10 minutes cooking time)
Per portion approx. 799 kcal/3341 kJ; 36 g P, 43 g F, 62 g CH

Puff pastry rolls with mince

Serves 4

1 pack frozen puff pastry (450 g), 1 onion, 1 garlic clove, 2 tomatoes, 1 tin kidney beans (400 g), 1 tin sweetcorn (400 g), 400 g assorted mince, 2 eggs, salt, pepper, $^1/_4$ tsp cayenne pepper, $^1/_2$ tsp sweet paprika powder, 2 tbsp freshly chopped chervil

1 Thaw the pastry. Peel and chop the onion and garlic. Wash, trim and dice the tomatoes. Drain the beans and sweetcorn. Mix together the vegetables, mince, 1 egg, spices and chervil. Separate the second egg.

2 Roll the pastry out into rectangles (reserving a little of the pastry) and brush the edges with beaten egg white. Spoon the mince onto the pastry and roll up. Make decorations from the remaining pastry, brush with egg white and decorate the rolls with them. Brush with beaten egg white.

3 Place the rolls on a baking sheet lined with parchment and bake in the oven at 200 °C (Gas Mark 6) for about 40 minutes. Then cut in slices and serve with salad. If necessary, cover with aluminium foil.

Preparation time: approx. 30 minutes (plus approx. 40 minutes baking time)
Per portion 1158 kcal/4864 kJ; approx. 42 g P, 62 g F, 109 g CH

Rissoles
with spicy pea purée

Serves 4

2 onions, $^1/_2$ bunch parsley, 500 g assorted mince, 1 egg yolk, 4 tbsp breadcrumbs,
2 tsp coarse-grain mustard, salt, pepper, 150 g ewe's milk cheese, 2 tbsp olive oil,
6 sprigs mint, 1 untreated lime, 1 tbsp butter, 1 kg frozen peas, 1 tsp vegetable stock

1 Peel the onions and chop finely. Wash the parsley, shake dry and chop the
leaves finely. Knead together the mince, half the chopped onion, egg yolk,
breadcrumbs, parsley and mustard. Season with salt and pepper. Drain the
cheese, cut into 12 cubes. Add the cheese to the mince mixture and form a rissole
round each cube.

2 Heat the oil in a large pan and brown the rissoles fiercely all over for 5 minutes,
then reduce the heat and fry for approx. a further 10 minutes over medium heat.

3 Meanwhile wash the mint, shake dry, reserve 1 sprig for garnishing, and pick
off the leaves from the remainder. Grate the rind of the lime, then cut in half and
squeeze out the juice. Melt the butter in a pan and fry the remaining onion until
transparent. Add the peas, stir in 200 ml water and the stock and bring to the boil.
Cover and simmer for approx. 5 minutes.

4 Drain the peas, reserving the stock. Add the lime juice and rind, mint and
5–6 tablespoons of pea stock to the peas. Purée with a hand blender and season
to taste with salt and pepper. Serve with the rissoles and garnish with the
remaining sprig of mint.

Preparation time: approx. 30 minutes
(plus approx. 15 minutes cooking time)
Per portion approx. 730 kcal/3066 kJ; 46 g P, 39 g F, 43 g CH

Zurich-style veal with rösti

Serves 4

For the veal: 1 onion, 1 garlic clove, 800 g veal (e.g. fillet, schnitzel or topside),
60 g clarified butter, 2 tbsp flour, 200 ml stock, 1 tbsp lemon juice, 200 ml cream, salt,
pepper; for the rösti: 800 g waxy potatoes boiled in their skins, left over from the
previous day, salt, pepper, 120 g butter

1 Peel the onion and garlic and chop very finely. Rinse the veal under cold running
water and pat dry. Cut the meat first in thin slices, then in narrow strips.

2 Heat the butter in a large pan and brown the meat on all sides, a portion at a time,
turning frequently, until it is brown all over. Remove from the pan and set aside.

3 Fry the onions and garlic in the same fat until transparent, dust with the flour, brown
briefly, and add the stock, lemon juice and cream. Return the meat to the pan and season
with salt and pepper. Warm for 5 minutes over low heat.

4 Peel the potatoes, grate and season well with salt and pepper. Melt 60g butter in a
pan, add the potatoes and smooth over. Fry the rösti until a brown crust forms on the
underside. Place a large plate on top of the pan, turn upside down and catch the rösti on
the plate. Melt a further 60 g butter in the pan, carefully slide the rösti from the plate
into the pan and fry on the other side. Cut in pieces and serve with the veal.

Preparation time: approx. 40 minutes (plus approx. 20 minutes frying time)
Per portion approx. 785 kcal/3287 kJ; 58 g P, 84 g F, 21 g CH

Meat loaf with olives

Serves 4

2 stale bread rolls, 75 g olives stuffed with peppers, 1 onion, 1 garlic clove, 1 tsp olive oil, $^1/_2$ bunch flat-leaf parsley, 1 sprig rosemary, 6 sprigs basil, 3 sprigs thyme, 750 g assorted mince, 2 eggs, 1 $^1/_2$ tsp salt, 1 tsp sweet paprika, $^1/_4$ tsp pepper

1 Pre-heat the oven to 200 °C (Gas Mark 6). Tear the rolls in rough pieces and soak in 125 ml water. Cut the olives in half crossways. Peel the onion and garlic and chop finely. Heat the olive oil in a pan and fry the onion until transparent.

2 Wash the herbs and pat dry with kitchen roll. Pick off the parsley and rosemary leaves and chop finely. Pick off the basil leaves and cut in fine strips. Strip the thyme leaves off the stalks.

3 Mix the mince with soaked bread, eggs, fried onion, garlic, olives and herbs. Season with salt, paprika and pepper and form the mixture into a long loaf shape.

4 Line a baking sheet with parchment and place the meat loaf on it. Bake on the middle shelf of the oven for about 1 hour. Leave to rest for 5 minutes, then cut in slices. Fried potatoes go very well with this.

Preparation time: approx. 25 minutes (plus approx. 1 hour cooking time)
Per portion approx. 560 kcal/2340 kJ; 42 g P, 38 g F, 13 g CH

Goulash

Serves 4

3 onions, 2 garlic cloves, 4 red peppers, 4 tbsp olive oil, 800 g stewing beef,
2 tbsp tomato paste, salt, pepper, 2 tsp sweet paprika powder, 450 ml meat stock,
60 g butter, 2 tbsp flour, 1 tsp hot paprika powder

1 Peel the onions and garlic cloves and chop. Trim the peppers, wash inside and out, dry and dice.

2 Heat the oil and brown the meat on all sides, a portion at a time. Remove from the pan and set aside. Fry the onions and garlic in the same fat until transparent. Add the meat and peppers. Stir in the tomato paste, season and after approx. 3 minutes add the stock. Cover and simmer for 1 1/2–2 hours over low heat.

3 30 minutes before the end of cooking time melt the butter in a small pan. Dust with flour and brown lightly. Add a ladleful of the goulash stock and stir until smooth. Add to the goulash. Continue simmering for approx. 20 minutes to thicken the goulash. Flavour with the hot paprika powder and serve with boiled potatoes or noodles.

Classic

Preparation time: approx. 30 minutes
(plus approx. 2 hours cooking time)
Per portion approx. 610 kcal/2550 kJ; 44 g P, 38 g F, 18 g CH

Stuffed peppers

Serves 4

1 stale bread roll, 4 red peppers, 2 onions, 4 garlic cloves, 50 g streaky bacon,
400 g assorted mince, 2 eggs, salt, pepper, 1 tsp sweet paprika powder,
$^1/_2$ tsp dried marjoram, 3 tbsp olive oil, 240 g chopped tomatoes (tinned),
1 pinch sugar

1 Pre-heat the oven to 200 °C (Gas Mark 6). Soak the bread roll in cold water.
Wash the peppers, cut off tops and remove the seeds and the white membranes.
Peel the onions and garlic and chop finely. Cut the bacon in small cubes.

2 Remove the roll from the water and squeeze well. In a bowl knead together the
bread roll, half the onions and garlic, eggs, herbs and spices. Spoon the mixture
into the peppers and put on the tops.

3 For the tomato sauce, heat the oil in a pan, sweat the remaining onions and
garlic and add the chopped tomatoes. Flavour with salt, pepper, a little paprika
powder and a pinch of sugar, bring slowly to the boil and transfer to an ovenproof
dish.

4 Arrange the stuffed peppers on the sauce and cook on the middle shelf of the
oven for approx. 40 minutes. Serve with white bread or rice.

Preparation time: approx. 20 minutes (plus approx. 50 minutes cooking time)
Per portion approx. 570 kcal/2380 kJ; 27 g P, 42 g F, 22 g CH

Pork schnitzel with leeks

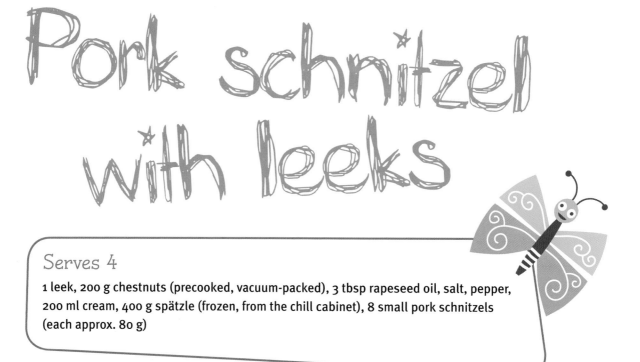

Serves 4

1 leek, 200 g chestnuts (precooked, vacuum-packed), 3 tbsp rapeseed oil, salt, pepper, 200 ml cream, 400 g spätzle (frozen, from the chill cabinet), 8 small pork schnitzels (each approx. 80 g)

1 Trim the leek, wash thoroughly, dry, cut in half lengthways and then in fine slices. Cut the chestnuts in quarters.

2 Heat 1 tablespoon of oil in a deep pan and lightly brown the leeks for approx. 4 minutes. Add the chestnuts, season with salt and pepper and add the cream. Simmer for approx. 4 minutes. Cook the spätzle in plenty of boiling salted water following the instructions on the packet. Drain thoroughly and add to the leeks.

3 Rinse the meat, pat dry, season with salt and pepper and, in a second pan, fry fiercely on both sides in the remaining oil. Add to the leeks and leave to draw for approx. 5 minutes. Serve on individual plates.

Preparation time: approx. 15 minutes (plus approx. 15 minutes cooking)
Per portion approx. 530 kcal/2220 kJ; 41 g P, 26 g F, 25 g CH

Wiener schnitzel

Serves 4

4 veal schnitzels (each 150 g), salt, pepper, 100 g flour, 3 eggs, 1 tbsp milk,
150 g breadcrumbs, 300 ml oil, 1 untreated lemon

1 Wash the veal, pat dry and beat very flat. Season with salt and pepper. Tip the flour onto a plate. In a deep dish beat together the eggs and milk. Tip the breadcrumbs onto a third plate.

2 Toss the schnitzels first in flour, then in egg and lastly in the breadcrumbs, making sure they stick firmly to the meat.

3 Heat the oil in a pan and, one at a time, fry the schnitzels for 3 minutes on each side. Remove from the pan and drain on kitchen roll.

4 Wash the lemon in hot water and cut in slices. Serve the schnitzels with potato salad and garnished with slices of lemon.

Preparation time: approx. 15 minutes (plus approx. 25 minutes frying time)
Per portion approx. 647 kcal/2927 kJ; 43 g P, 35 g F, 48 g CH

Beef roulades

Serves 4

2 onions, 4–8 gherkins, 4 thin slices of beef (each 150 g), 3–4 tsp medium-hot mustard, 4 slices uncooked ham, salt, black pepper, 1 leek, 2 carrots, $^1/_4$ celeriac, 3 tbsp sunflower oil, 3 tbsp flour, 400 ml meat stock, 1 tsp dried marjoram

1 Peel the onions and chop very finely. Set half aside for later. Cut the gherkins in small cubes. Spread the meat with mustard, top each with a slice of ham and then with onions and gherkins and season with salt and pepper. Roll up the beef and tie with kitchen string or fasten with roulade clips.

2 Trim the leek and wash thoroughly. Then cut in strips diagonally. Wash the carrots, cut off the root and stalk ends and peel. Cut the carrots first in lengthways strips and then dice. Trim and peel the celeriac and cut in small cubes.

3 Heat the oil in a stew pan, Brown the roulades on all sides and remove from the pan. Sweat the remaining diced onions and vegetables in the fat for a few minutes, then return the roulades to the pan and dust with 1 tablespoon of flour. Add the meat stock, cover and simmer the roulades for approx. 1 hour.

4 Remove the roulades from the pan, cover with aluminium foil and keep warm. Strain the meat juices and reduce a little. Mix the remaining flour with a little cold water and stir into the boiling meat juices. Bring to the boil and season to taste with salt, pepper and a little marjoram.

Preparation time: approx. 40 minutes (plus approx. 1 hour cooking time)
Per portion approx. 310 kcal/1300 kJ; 33 g P, 14 g F, 8 g CH

Eggy bread

lemon-flavoured

Serves 4

250 ml milk, 1 tsp grated rind of 1 untreated lemon, 3 tbsp sugar, 1 tsp cinnamon, 4 slices stale white bread, 4 eggs, 60 g butter

1 In a pan, bring the milk to a boil with the lemon rind, sugar and cinnamon, then leave to cool.

2 Soak the slices of bread in the cooled milk for 5 minutes.

3 In a deep dish beat the eggs until foamy. Remove the bread from the milk and toss in the beaten egg.

4 Melt the butter in a pan and fry the bread on both sides until golden brown and crisp.

Tasty

Preparation time: approx. 15 minutes (plus approx. 15 minutes cooking time and approx. 10 minutes frying time)
Per portion approx. 357 kcal/1499 kJ; 12 g P, 22 g F, 26 g CH

Traditional cherry pudding

Serves 4

500 ml milk, 6 stale bread rolls, 100 g butter, 75 g sugar, 4 eggs, 750 g cherries, 1 pinch cinnamon, 1 pinch salt, butter for greasing

1 Pre-heat the oven to 200 °C (Gas Mark 6). Warm the milk. Cut the rolls in slices and soak in the warm milk. Mix 75 g butter with the sugar. Separate the eggs, add the yolks to the butter and sugar mixture and beat to a foam.

2 Mix the bread with the milk and egg mixture. Wash the cherries, remove the stalks and stones and add to the mixture along with the cinnamon. Beat the egg whites stiff and fold in to the mixture.

3 Grease an ovenproof dish with a little butter. Tip the mixture into it and top with flakes of the remaining butter. Bake in the oven for about 50 minutes.

Preparation time: approx. 20 minutes
(plus approx. 50 minutes baking time)
Per portion approx. 647 kcal/2927 kJ; 43 g P, 35 g F, 48 g CH

Yeast dumplings

with vanilla sauce

Serves 4

For the yeast dumplings: 500 g flour, 30 g yeast, 160 g sugar, 750 ml milk, 2 eggs, salt, 50 g butter; for the vanilla sauce: 6 egg yolks, 150 g sugar, 350 ml milk, pith of 1 vanilla pod, 150 ml cream

1 Sift the flour into a bowl and make a well in the middle. Crumble the yeast and mix with 1 teaspoon of sugar and 50 ml warm milk. Pour this mixture into the well in the flour, dust with flour, cover and leave to rise in a warm place for 15 minutes.

2 Next mix the pre-dough with 180 ml milk, the eggs and 50 g sugar and knead by hand to an elastic dough. It should come away easily from the hands. Cover the dough and leave to rise again for 30 minutes.

3 Knead the dough thoroughly. Moisten your hands and form about 8 dumplings and leave to rise for a further 15 minutes. In a large, shallow pan heat the remaining milk with the remaining sugar, salt and butter. Drop the dumplings into it, cover and steam for about 20 minutes.

4 For the sauce, mix the egg yolks with the sugar and stir until foamy over a hot bain-marie. Gradually add the milk, vanilla pith and cream and stir the sauce over moderate heat until creamy. Serve the dumplings with the vanilla sauce. Fresh berries go well with this.

Preparation time: approx. 40 minutes (plus approx. 1 hour rising time and approx. 20 minutes cooking time)
Per portion approx. 847 kcal/3557 kJ; 23 g P, 21 g F, 137 g CH

Classic

Potato and poppy seed dumplings

Serves 4

500 g floury potatoes, salt, 60 g butter, 1 egg, 150 g spelt flour, 200 g ground poppy seeds, 50 g sugar, 1 tbsp milk, 1 tbsp brown sugar, icing sugar for dusting

1 Boil the potatoes in a little salted water for about 20 minutes, drain and peel while still hot. Mash in a potato ricer and knead to a firm dough with 50 g butter, salt, egg and flour.

2 Form the potato dough into rolls the thickness of your thumb and cut in finger-length pieces. Taper to a point at each end. Cook in boiling salted water for about 10 minutes, then drain, rinse in cold water and leave to drip. Pre-heat the oven to 180 °C (Gas Mark 4).

3 In a pan, lightly toast the ground poppy seeds with the sugar and remainder of the butter.

4 Add the milk and dumplings to the pan and shake gently. Sprinkle with the brown sugar. Bake the dumplings in the oven for about 20 minutes. Serve dusted with icing sugar.

Preparation time: approx. 30 minutes (plus cooking time).
Per portion approx. 650 kcal/2730 kJ; 18 g P, 36 g F, 62 g CH

Traditional
Kaiserschmarrn

Serves 4

50 g raisins, 3 tbsp apple juice, 4 fresh eggs, salt, 4 tbsp sugar, 1 packet vanilla sugar, 100 g wheat flour, 200 ml milk, 70 g cold butter, 50 g almond nibs, a little icing sugar for dusting

1 Rinse the raisins and leave to drain. Soak in a cup of apple juice.

2 Separate the eggs. Beat the whites with 1 pinch salt until stiff. Drizzle in 2 tablespoons of sugar and continue beating until the mixture has stiffened again. Beat the egg yolks to a thick foam with the remaining sugar and the vanilla sugar.

3 Gradually stir the flour and milk into the egg yolk mixture. Mix in the raisins. Lastly fold in the beaten egg whites.

4 Melt half the butter. Pour the batter into the pan, fry until golden brown and turn over.

5 Using 2 forks, pull the pancake into rough pieces. Add the remaining butter and the almonds. Continue frying until the pieces are golden brown on all sides. Serve dusted with icing sugar.

Preparation time: approx. 15 minutes (plus approx. 15 minutes cooking time)
Per portion approx. 480 kcal/2010 kJ; 15 g P, 30 g F, 33 g CH

Filled yeast buns

Serves 4–6

500 g flour, 200 ml milk, 28 g yeast, 70 g sugar, 1 pinch salt, 170 g butter, grated rind of ¹/₂ untreated lemon, 2 eggs, 50 g plum jam, flour for the worktop, fat for greasing

1 Sift the flour into a bowl, make a well in the middle and add 100 ml lukewarm milk, the crumbled yeast, 2 teaspoons of sugar and a pinch of salt. Dust around the rim with flour, cover and leave to rise in a warm place for 15 minutes.

2 Melt 70 g butter and mix with the remaining milk, the remaining sugar, the lemon rind and the eggs, add to the pre-dough and, working from the centre out, knead with the flour to give a firm yeast dough. Cover the dough and leave to rise in a warm place for 30 minutes.

3 On a floured worktop, roll out the dough to a thickness of about 2 cm and cut in squares of 6 x 6 cm. Place a teaspoon of jam on each square of dough and form into balls.

4 Melt the remaining butter and roll the dough balls in it, then arrange them close together in a buttered ovenproof dish. Cover with a cloth and leave to rise again until the buns have doubled in volume. Pre-heat the oven to 200 °C (Gas Mark 6).

5 Brush the buns with a little of the remaining melted butter and bake in the oven for about 40 minutes until golden brown. Brush once again with butter during baking. Vanilla sauce goes well with these.

Preparation time: approx. 30 minutes (plus approx. 90 minutes rising time and approx. 40 minutes baking time)
Per portion approx. 616 kcal/2587 kJ; 12 g P, 27 g F, 78 g CH

Party food

The recipes in this chapter are for the special days in the year. Your cucumber crocodiles, rainbow cakes or monster muffins will be a smash hit at any children's party and ensure unforgettable party fun. Find your inspiration here.

Pizza cobra

Makes 1 pizza snake

For the dough: 15 g fresh yeast, sugar, 250 g wheat flour, 1 tbsp olive oil, 1 tsp salt;
for the topping: 1 onion, 1 garlic clove, 1 tsp oil, 250 g chopped tomatoes (tinned),
$^1/_2$ bunch oregano, 150 g cooked ham, 1 yellow pepper, salt, pepper, 250 g mozzarella,
30 g Parmesan; other: flour for the worktop, 1 egg and milk for brushing, 2 olives for the
eyes, 1 piece red pepper for the tongue

1 Crumble the yeast in 100 ml lukewarm water. Mix in a pinch of sugar and 1 tablespoon of
flour, cover and leave this pre-dough to rest for 15 minutes.

2 Add the pre-dough to the remaining flour and mix together, then add the oil and salt and
knead the dough thoroughly. Cover with a damp cloth and leave to rise in a warm place until
it has doubled in volume. This will take approx. 1 hour.

3 Meanwhile, peel and chop the onion and garlic clove. Brown lightly in the oil. Add the
chopped tomatoes and simmer for approx. 15 minutes without the lid, then remove from the
heat.

4 Wash the oregano, shake dry and chop the leaves. Dice the ham. Trim, wash and dry the
pepper and dice this too. Mix these ingredients into the tomato sauce and season with salt
and pepper. Cut the mozzarella in slices and grate the Parmesan.

5 Pre-heat the oven to 200 °C (Gas Mark 6). Line a baking sheet with baking paper. Knead
the dough thoroughly on a floured worktop, set aside a handful of dough for the head and
form the remainder into a long roll. Roll this out with a rolling pin.

6 Arrange the dough on the baking sheet in the shape of a snake. Roll the head portion
into a pear shape and attach to the front of the body. Using your fingers press the body out
towards the sides and form a little raised edge all round. Beat the egg with a little milk and
brush the head and sides with it.

7 Spread the tomato sauce over the body, top with mozzarella and sprinkle with Parmesan.
Bake for approx. 25 minutes. Pin the olives on for the eyes with 2 toothpicks and cut a little
slit for the mouth. Cut a triangle out of one end of the piece of pepper and insert the other
end in the slit to form the forked tongue.

Preparation time approx. 45 minutes (plus approx. 60 minutes rising time and approx. 25 minutes baking time)
Per pizza snake approx. 1990 kcal/8320 kJ; 121 g P, 82 g F, 188 g CH

Pizza whirls

Serves 4

For the dough: 300 g flour, 1 packet dried yeast, 1 pinch sugar, 100 g diced processed cheese with herbs, salt; for the filling: 1 onion, 2 tbsp olive oil, 300 g assorted mince, salt, pepper, 400 g peeled tomatoes (tinned), 2 tbsp tomato paste, 1 tbsp thyme, 50 g grated Parmesan; other: flour for the worktop

1 Sift the flour into a bowl. Make a well in the middle. Add the yeast. Sprinkle with a pinch of sugar. Warm 125 ml water. Cut the cheese in small cubes. Spread $^1/_2$ a teaspoon of salt and the cheese around the edge of the bowl. Add the lukewarm water. Knead to a smooth dough first with a hand mixer, then with your hands. Cover and leave to rise in a warm place for approx. 60 minutes.

2 Peel the onion and chop finely. Heat the oil and fry the onions until transparent. Add the mince. Season with salt and pepper and fry until crumbly. Add the tomatoes with the juice and the tomato paste. Reduce with the lid off. Flavour with the thyme.

3 Pre-heat the oven to 220 °C (Gas Mark 7). Line 2 baking sheets with parchment. On a floured worktop, roll the dough out to a rectangle approx. 20 x 30 cm. Place the dough on a tea towel. Sprinkle with Parmesan. Spread the sauce over the dough, leaving the edges free. Roll the dough up lengthways with the aid of the cloth and press the "seam" together firmly.

4 Cut the roll in 12 equally thick slices. Place on the baking sheet with the cut surface down. Leave to rise for a further 10 minutes. Bake for approx. 20 minutes.

Preparation time: approx. 30 minutes
(plus approx. 1 hour and 10 minutes to rise and approx. 20 minutes for baking)
Per slice approx. 210 kcal/880 kJ; 10 g P, 10 g F, 19 g CH

Frankfurter octopus

For 1 octopus plate

1 long frankfurter; other: 1 portion chips, ketchup and mayonnaise for decoration, frying oil

1 Make 2 cuts in each end of the frankfurter to within approx. 1 cm of the middle, with the cuts intersecting at right angles, to form the 8 legs. When you have cut into one end, cut into the other end so that the cuts do not match (i.e. the frankfurter – apart from the uncut middle – must not be divided exactly in four).

2 Deep fry the frankfurter octopus in hot oil until golden brown and arrange on a plate of chips. Decorate with ketchup and mayonnaise.

Preparation time: approx. 5 minutes (plus approx. 5 minutes frying time)
Per octopus plate approx. 620 kcal/2590 kJ; 15 g P, 48 g F, 33 g CH

Spider crackers

Makes 10

7 tbsp cream cheese, 20 round crackers, 30 pretzel sticks, 7 green olives, stuffed with peppers

Hit at Halloween

1 Spread the cream cheese on 10 crackers, reserving 1 tablespoon. Break the pretzel sticks in half and give each cracker 3 legs each side, laying the pretzel sticks on the cream cheese. Now lay another cracker on top of each and press gently in place.

2 Cut the olives in 20 slices. For the eyes, stick 2 olive slices in place on each cracker with a little cream cheese. If you like you can also paint a mouth on the spiders with cream cheese.

3 Alternatively the crackers can of course be filled with other spreadable ingredients.

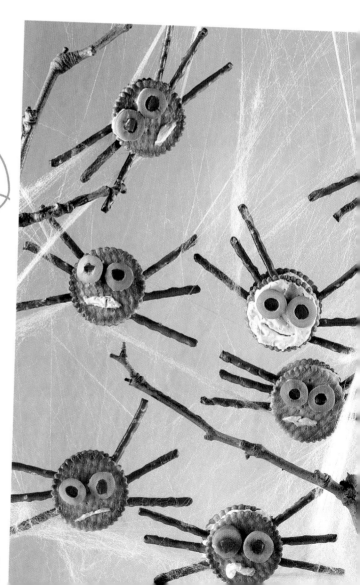

Preparation time: approx. 10 minutes
Per spider approx. 50 kcal/210 kJ; 1 g P, 3 g F, 4 g CH

Cucumber crocodile

Makes 1 crocodile

1 thick cucumber, approx. 250 g red grapes, approx. 250 g Gouda, 1 slice salami,
1 mini-mozzarella, 2 small capers

Decorative

1 Wash and dry the cucumber and level off one long side so that the cucumber
will lie firmly. Divide the slice you cut off into 4 equal pieces and shape into
triangles. Give one side of each a zigzag edge and later position them by the
cucumber as crocodile feet.

2 Make a horizontal cut into the pointed end of the cucumber approx. 10 cm deep.
Then with a sharp knife cut the upper and lower edges into jagged teeth. Put the
cucumber on a serving dish.

3 Wash and dry the grapes. Cut the Gouda in slices approx. 5 mm thick and cut
triangles out of them. Roll up the slice of salami and insert in the crocodile's
mouth for the tongue. If the mouth is not open wide enough, jam a grape in behind
it. Cut the mozzarella ball in half for the eyes and put a caper on each for the
pupils. Fix the eyes in place behind the nose with toothpicks.

4 Spear a cheese triangle on top of a grape on toothpicks and arrange these in
three rows along the crocodile's body.

Preparation time approx. 30 minutes
Per crocodile approx. 940 kcal/3930 kJ; 77 g P, 49 g F, 44 g CH

Cheese beetles

Makes 8

3 tbsp mayonnaise, $^1/_2$ tsp mustard, salt, pepper, 8 round slices of pumpernickel, 8 small round cheeses, 8 chive blades, 16 small capers, 1 tbsp ketchup; other: mayonnaise to fix the capers

1 Mix the mayonnaise with the mustard and season well with salt and pepper. Spread over the pumpernickel and arrange the cheeses on top. If the pumpernickel rounds are too big, trim to the size of the cheese.

2 Cut the cheeses along the middle, without cutting right through, and bend the halves slightly apart. Wash the chives, shake dry and cut the blades in half. On each beetle, insert 2 chive blades for feelers into the mayonnaise and mustard between the undivided section of cheese and the pumpernickel. Above this put two little dabs of mayonnaise on the cheese and press one caper in each for the eyes. Decorate the wing cases with spots of ketchup. It is easiest to do this with a wooden skewer or a toothpick.

Preparation time: approx. 20 minutes
Per beetle approx. 80 kcal/330 kJ; 3 g P, 7 g F, 3 g CH

Quick

Frankfurter caterpillars

Makes 12

1 jar mini frankfurters in strings (190 g), a few nice lettuce leaves, 6 mini mozzarella balls, 6 cherry tomatoes, 1 sprig curly parsley, a little cress, 1 tsp ketchup, 1 tsp mayonnaise, toothpicks

1 Drain the frankfurters in a sieve and cut the strings in 12 sections. These can be of different lengths. Wash the lettuce leaves, pat dry and arrange on a serving dish. Arrange the frankfurter strings on top.

2 Drain the mozzarella balls and pat dry. Wash and dry the cherry tomatoes and remove the stalk ends. Wash the parsley, pat dry and pick off the leaves. Carefully cut the cress, wash and pat dry.

3 With a toothpick, bore small holes in the tomatoes and insert 1–2 parsley leaves in each as tufts of hair. Bore small holes in the mozzarella balls as well and insert small tufts of cress.

4 For the caterpillar faces, paint the mozzarella balls with ketchup and the tomatoes with mayonnaise. Do this by dipping a toothpick in ketchup or mayonnaise and carefully dabbing 2 eyes and a mouth on the front. Then place the decorated mozzarella balls and tomatoes on the strings of frankfurters as caterpillar heads.

Preparation time: approx. 15 minutes
Per caterpillar approx. 130 kcal/540 kJ; 7 g P, 11 g F, 1 g CH

Crocodile bake

Makes 1 crocodile

For the filling: 2 stale bread rolls, 1 onion, 1 tsp oil, 1 bunch parsley, 100 g Gouda, 1 kg minced beef, 2 eggs, 150 g cream cheese, $^1/_2$ tube tomato paste, salt, pepper; other: 8 sheets frozen puff pastry, 1 egg, 1 tbsp cream, 2 tbsp chopped pistachios for sprinkling, 2 star anise for the eyes, flour for the worktop

1 Soak the bread rolls in lukewarm water for approx. 10 minutes. Peel the onion, chop and sweat in the oil until transparent. Set aside. Wash the parsley, shake dry and chop the leaves. Grate the Gouda. Pre-heat the oven to 180 °C (Gas Mark 4) and line a baking sheet with parchment. Squeeze the moisture out of the rolls and put in a bowl. Add the onion, parsley, Gouda, mince, eggs, cream cheese and tomato paste, season with salt and pepper and knead together. Take 2 tablespoons of the mixture and roll into balls. Set aside for making the eyes later.

2 Thaw the puff pastry. Roll out 6 sheets on a floured worktop. Arrange slightly overlapping in a square lying diagonally on the baking sheet. Spoon the mince mixture on top and form one end into a roll tapering to a point for the crocodile's tail. At the thicker end, which will form the head, press the balls of mixture on the right and left where the eyes will be. Now fold the pastry over the mince so that the filling is completely covered. Press together and cut away the excess. Form this into 4 rolls and attach to the crocodile for the legs. Make notches in them with the back of a knife.

3 Roll out the remaining pastry sheets a little. Cut in triangles and arrange along the crocodile's back for scales. If desired press on 2 bulges above the eyes.

4 Beat the egg with the cream and brush the crocodile with the mixture. Lastly, sprinkle the back with chopped pistachios and stick on 2 star anise for the eyes. Bake on the middle shelf for approx. 60 minutes. If the pastry goes too brown, cover the crocodile with aluminium foil.

Preparation time: approx. 30 minutes (plus approx. 60 minutes baking time)
Per crocodile approx. 4700 kcal/19650 kJ; 293 g P, 317 g F, 173 g CH

Toadstools

Makes 10

10 eggs, 1 box cress, 5 medium tomatoes, 1 tube mayonnaise

1 Prick the eggs and hard boil for approx. 10 minutes. Then drain and plunge in cold water. Leave to cool completely.

2 Cut the cress, rinse carefully under running water and pat dry. Then arrange decoratively on a serving dish. Wash and dry the tomatoes and carefully cut out the stalk ends. Then cut the tomatoes in half and hollow out with a teaspoon. Pat dry with kitchen roll.

3 Peel the eggs and, with a knife, cut the thick ends level so the eggs will stand firm. Then arrange them on the serving dish decorated with the cress. Place the tomato halves on top and paint spots on the toadstools with mayonnaise.

Preparation time: approx. 15 minutes (plus approx. 10 minutes cooking time and approx. 20 minutes to cool)
Per toadstool approx. 125 kcal/527 kJ; 8 g P, 10 g F, 1 g CH

Pharaohs
in blankets

Serves 4

4 sheets frozen puff pastry, 8 frankfurters, 1 egg yolk, 1 tbsp milk, coarse sea salt for sprinkling; other: flour for the worktop, mayonnaise and 16 black peppercorns for the eyes

1 Pre-heat the oven to 200 °C (Gas Mark 6). Line a baking sheet with parchment and sprinkle with water. Thaw the pastry sheets, roll out slightly on a floured worktop and cut in half lengthways. With a sharp knife cut each half sheet in approx. 3 strips.

2 Prick the frankfurters several times with a fork so they will not split, then wrap them in the pastry strips, leaving the upper end open for the head but making sure there is some pastry under the head – maybe as a pillow. Arrange the pharaohs on the baking sheet.

3 Beat together the egg yolk and milk. Brush the pastry with the egg yolk and sprinkle with a pinch of coarse sea salt. Bake on the middle shelf of the oven for approx. 10 minutes. Allow to cool a little, then with a little mayonnaise stick 2 black peppercorns on each head for the eyes and draw a mouth.

Preparation time: approx. 10 minutes (plus approx. 10 minutes thawing time and approx. 10 minutes baking time)
Per portion approx. 260 kcal/1090 kJ; 9 g P, 22 g F, 7 g CH

Rissole faces

Makes 12 rissoles with various decorations

For the rissole mixture: 3 three stale bread rolls, 1 bunch parsley, 4 tbsp pine nuts, 4 onions, 2 garlic cloves, 5 tbsp oil, 1 kg assorted mince, 3 eggs, salt, pepper, sweet paprika powder; other: 4 green olives stuffed with peppers, mayonnaise in a tube, 4 baby sweetcorn in a jar, 4 curly lettuce leaves, 4 slices white bread, ketchup, 2 cherry tomatoes, 4 black olives, 1 red and 1 yellow pepper, 8 black or red peppercorns

1 Cut the rolls in pieces and soak in a little cold water. Wash the parsley, shake dry and chop the leaves. Toast the pine nuts in a dry pan until golden brown, chop coarsely and tip into a bowl with the parsley. Peel and chop the onions and garlic cloves. Fry in 1 tablespoon of oil until transparent, then add to the parsley. Squeeze out the rolls and add to the bowl. Add the mince, eggs, salt, pepper and paprika powder and knead into a dough. Form 12 rissoles and fry in the hot oil on both sides until brown and crisp.

2 For 4 creepy rissoles, cut the green olives in half. With mayonnaise stick 2 half olives on each rissole for eyes. With a sharp knife cut a hole in the middle of the rissole and insert a baby sweetcorn for the nose.

3 For 4 clown rissoles, place the rissoles on curly lettuce leaves. Cut 2 square slices of white bread in half diagonally to form the biggest possible triangles. Spread with mayonnaise, decorate with 4–5 spots of ketchup up the central line, and arrange above the rissoles as clowns' hats. Cut each of the remaining slices of bread into 4 triangles and arrange below the rissoles as bow ties, covering the join with a piece of cherry tomato. For the eyes, cut the black olives in half and stick to the rissoles with mayonnaise. Paint the mouth and nose with mayonnaise and ketchup.

4 For 4 crab rissoles, trim, wash and dry the peppers and cut 16 equally long, thin strips from each. Make 4 holes in each side of the rissoles and insert 4 strips of pepper for the legs. Paint the eyes with mayonnaise and peppercorns and the mouth with ketchup.

Preparation time: approx. 40 minutes (plus approx. 12 minutes frying time)
Per rissole approx. 370 kcal/1550 kJ; 20 g P, 26 g F, 15 g CH

Monster muffins

Makes 12

125 g soft butter, 200 g sugar, 1 packet vanilla sugar, 3 eggs, 300 g flour, 1 packet baking powder, 125 ml milk, 100 g chocolate drops, 125 g marzipan, 200 g icing sugar, 100 g grated coconut, blue food colouring, 6 chocolate chip cookies

1 For the muffins, pre-heat the oven to 180 °C (Gas Mark 4). Line a muffin tin with paper cases. Beat the softened butter with the sugar and vanilla sugar until foamy. Gradually mix in the eggs.

2 Mix the flour and baking powder and sift into the egg mixture. Then add the milk and mix to a smooth dough. Set aside 24 chocolate drops and mix the remainder into the dough.

3 Spoon the mixture into the muffin tins and bake on the middle shelf of the oven for 20–25 minutes. Remove from the oven, leave in the tins to rest for a short time, then leave to cool completely on a wire rack.

4 For the eyes, knead the marzipan together with 75 g icing sugar and roll into 24 small, round balls. Press the reserved chocolate drops into the marzipan eyes for the pupils.

5 Tip the grated coconut into a bowl and colour with a little blue food colouring. It is best to wear rubber gloves while doing this. Then spread the grated coconut on a baking sheet lined with parchment and leave to dry. Then put them back in a bowl.

6 Make a viscous icing with the remaining icing sugar, blue food colouring and a little water. Brush over the tops of the muffins (reserving a little of the icing for the eyes) and dip the muffins head-first in the blue grated coconut. With a sharp knife cut a slit in each muffin and insert half a chocolate chip cookie as a mouth. Stick the eyes on the muffins with a little icing and leave to dry.

Preparation time: approx. 45 minutes (plus approx. 20 minutes baking time, approx. 30 minutes to cool and approx. 3 hours to dry)
Per muffin approx. 530 kcal/2220 kJ; 8 g P, 24 g F, 69 g CH

Sweet beer
with vanilla froth

Looks quite real

Makes approx. 8 glasses

2 packets lemon jelly mix (for a total of 1 litre fluid), 200 g sugar, 1 tin apricots (425 ml), 400 ml cream, 2 packets vanilla sugar

1 In a pan, mix together the jelly powder, 1 litre of cold water and the sugar. Leave to stand for a short time. Drain the apricots in a sieve, retaining the juice. Refrigerate the juice for use later. Dice the apricots and put half of them into glasses.

2 Heat the jelly mix following the instructions on the packet but do not boil. Allow to cool slightly and pour half into the glasses on top of the apricots. Allow to cool, then refrigerate for approx. 2 hours, until the jelly has set. Keep the remaining jelly at room temperature.

3 As soon as the jelly in the refrigerator has set, add the remaining diced apricots, then pour in the remaining jelly. Preferably refrigerate overnight.

4 Shortly before serving beat the cream and vanilla sugar to a stiff froth. Add just enough of the reserved apricot juice to make the froth nice and creamy. Add to the glasses to look like beer froth and serve immediately.

Preparation time: approx. 25 minutes (plus approx. 12 hours chilling time)
Per portion approx. 300 kcal/1250 kJ; 5 g P, 15 g F, 37 g CH

Carrot cake

Serves 16

400 g carrots, 8 eggs, 250 g sugar, 200 g ground hazelnuts, 200 g ground almonds, 60 g cornflour, 1 tsp cinnamon, juice and grated rind of 1 lemon, salt, 200 g icing sugar, 3 tbsp lemon juice, 12 marzipan carrots, 20 g chopped pistachios, butter for greasing

1 Wash, trim and peel the carrots. Grate finely and set aside. Pre-heat the oven to 175 °C (Gas Mark 4). Line a springform cake tin (26 cm diameter) with parchment and grease the sides.

2 Separate the eggs. Beat the egg yolks and sugar to a foam. Fold in the carrots.

3 Mix the hazelnuts with the almonds and cornflour, stir into the egg and carrot mixture, then add the cinnamon and the lemon rind and juice.

4 Beat the egg whites with a pinch of salt until stiff and mix gently with the egg and carrot mixture. Transfer the mixture to the springform tin and smooth over.

5 Bake the cake on the middle shelf of the oven for about 1 hour and 10 minutes. If the cake goes too brown, cover with aluminium foil. After about 60 minutes test to see if it is ready. Prod it with a wooden skewer and if no mixture sticks to the skewer the cake is ready. Let the cake cool and release from the cake tin.

6 For the icing, mix the icing sugar with the lemon juice and brush over the cake. Decorate with marzipan carrots and pistachios.

Preparation time: approx. 30 minutes (plus approx. 70 minutes baking time and approx. 40 minutes for cooling)
Per portion approx. 282 kcal/1184 kJ; 10 g P, 16 g F, 26 g CH

Spider chocolate cake

Makes 1 cake (26 cm diameter springform tin)

250 g semisweet chocolate, 40 g butter, 6 eggs, salt, 160 g sugar, 1 packet vanilla sugar, 100 g flour, 1 tsp baking powder, 200 g blackcurrant jelly, 150 ml grape juice; other: butter for greasing, 250 g white cake coating, red tube icing, icing sugar for fastening, 1–2 liquorice wheels, 5 liquorice drops

1 Pre-heat the oven to 180 °C (Gas Mark 4). Grease a springform cake tin with butter. Break the chocolate in pieces and melt with the butter in a hot bain-marie, then remove from the heat. Separate the eggs. Beat the egg whites stiff with a pinch of salt and refrigerate for later use. Beat the egg yolks, sugar and vanilla sugar to a foam. Slowly stir in the chocolate while it is still just liquid. Mix the flour and baking powder together and sift over the mixture. Stir in, then fold in the egg whites in 3 stages. Transfer to the cake tin, smooth over and bake on the middle shelf of the oven for approx. 50 minutes. Leave to cool completely on a wire rack.

2 Next, cut the cake in half horizontally. Warm the blackcurrant jelly until it is runny. Spread over the bottom layer of the cake and place the other layer on top. Prick the surface with a toothpick and soak with grape juice. Melt the white cake coating in a bain-marie and cover the cake with a thick layer. Leave to dry.

3 With red tube icing draw a spider's web on the cake. Mix a little icing sugar with a little water until viscous. Unroll the liquorice wheels and separate the two strings. Cut the strings into a total of 15 equal pieces. Stick 3–4 at a time to the underside of a liquorice drop with a little icing and position them on the cake. If desired, paint eyes on the spiders with red tube icing.

Preparation time: approx. 60 minutes (plus approx. 50 minutes baking time and approx. 1 hour cooling time)
Per cake approx. 4920 kcal/25570 kJ; 91 g P, 183 g F, 648 g CH

Rainbow cake

Makes 1 mini loaf cake

For the dough: 50 g butter, 50 g sugar, 1 egg, 60 g flour, $^1/_2$ tsp baking powder, 1 tbsp milk, $^1/_4$ packet vanilla sauce powder, $^1/_4$ packet cherry jelly mix, $^1/_4$ packet mixed fruit jelly; for decoration: 80 g icing sugar, multicoloured sugar sprinkles and beads; other: butter for greasing

1 Preheat the oven to 180 °C (Gas Mark 4). Grease a 15-cm mini loaf tin with butter. For the dough, work the butter until soft. Gradually add the sugar, then the egg and mix together. Mix the flour and baking powder and mix in alternately with the milk.

2 Divide the dough in three. Mix one part with the vanilla sauce powder, the second with the cherry jelly powder and the third with the mixed fruit jelly powder. Transfer the three parts to the loaf tin in layers, starting with the yellow dough and finishing with green. Bake for approx. 40 minutes. Leave to cool briefly in the tin, then remove and leave to cool completely.

3 For the decoration, mix the icing sugar with a little water to give a smooth icing and spread over the cake. Sprinkle with the sugar sprinkles and beads while the icing is still soft and press in gently. Leave the icing to set firm.

Tip:
The three layers of dough will form this pretty pattern almost by themselves during baking. However, the results will look a bit different every time you bake one. You can also create a pretty pattern by pulling a fork in a spiral through the layers of dough.

Preparation time: approx. 25 minutes (plus approx. 40 minutes baking time and approx. 30 minutes for cooling)
Per cake approx. 4490 kcal/18770 kJ; 83 g P, 293 g F, 383 g CH

Index by chapters

Party food

Alphabetical index